LIFE'S LESSONS FROM BEHIND THE BADGE

WE OUGHT NOT to look back unless it is to derive useful lessons from past errors, or for the purpose of profiting by dear-bought experience.

GEORGE WASHINGTON

ISBN 0-9664278-0-7

Published in the United States
by Motivational Speakers Institute.

Printed by
Prestige Press, Inc., North Little Rock, Arkansas.

YOU WILL LEARN LESSONS FROM . . .

... A former president and vice president of the USA and a rookie police officer

... A body guard to the stars

... An inmate in the death chamber and his amazing last words to an execution team member

... A police officer named Robin Hood and the humor behind the badge

... Inmates and their unbelievable lawsuits

... A car chase where the suspects chase the cops

... Leaders who make decisions and encourage officers like you won't believe

... A drug addict who dreams of flying high at NASA

... A high school senior who begs for help from those he called "Pig"

... The Bloody Badges of 1984

... Train crash victim, coroner, wrecker driver, suicide victim and much, much more

... A death row religious conversion

... A hospital morgue and the rookie

WHAT OTHER PEOPLE ARE SAYING ABOUT THIS OUTSTANDING BOOK

"As a retired police supervisor for the Phoenix (Arizona) Police Department, I've experienced the loss of fellow officers, many of whom were close personal friends. I have also responded to similar emergencies as are depicted in the book. Though our stories are similar, I was unable to put your book down. I highly recommend your work to both civilians and officers."

Gary G. Mulleneaux
Sgt. Phoenix Police Department (Ret.)

"These stories are sad, funny, and true. One cannot possibly read these stories without being touched by the spirit of the souls remembered in them. In his own way, then, Chief Campbell has made their sacrifice immortal."

Dr. Jim Moore, Ed.D.,
Training Resources Associates, Inc.
Ridgeland, Mississippi

• •

ACKNOWLEDGMENTS

First of all, I would like to thank my wife, Debi, whose continued encouragement to start and finish this book is one of the main reasons this book is in your hands today; and

Barbara J. Stringer and Ike Thompson, for all their help and hard work in editing this book.

And Teresa Funderburg for her many hours of dedication in transforming my hand-written work into a type-written manuscript.

And last, but not least, my former instructors, supervisors and fellow officers, whose influence helped mold me into the officer I am today. After twenty years behind the badge, may they still take pride in knowing that the lessons they taught me did not get erased from the chalk board of my mind.

DEDICATION PAGE

This book is dedicated to fifteen of my former law enforcement students who have given their lives in the line of duty. All of us gave some, but some, gave all. May those who read this book respect you and other police and correction officers who have given *their* lives to protect them in the line of duty.

CONTENTS

CHAPTER 1

CHAPTER 7

SERVICE

CHAPTER 8

GUARDING THE STARS

CHAPTER 9

ETHICS

CHAPTER 10

LEADERSHIP

CHAPTER 11

THE KIDS

CHAPTER 12

HUMOR

FORWARD

"Once I began reading this book, I could not put it down. I read it until the early morning hours. My advice to you is to start reading this book early, so that you can still get to sleep on time.

Each chapter and story provides a winning formula for us all. From this book, we learn how to gain strength from our human tragedy experiences. Chief Campbell teaches that we need not despair from such human suffering. Instead, we can gain more freedom and happiness by taking with us life's lessons so that we face each day with more gratitude for what we have, greater thanksgiving for the grace we received to survive and a bright new hope each day for the life we have because somebody else is always less fortunate.

This book caused me to reflect and learn again from my adversities. This time, however, it was without pain. I remember parachuting out of an airplane minutes before it crashed and picking up the pieces of my friends who remained in the plane, The rescue workers arrived at the scene but went into shock after vomiting, violently. I asked myself, 'What could be done?' Only my friend and I could stomach the chore. These were our friends; we could not leave them to be rescued by strangers. Even though they could never thank us, we helped them because we loved them. It was the right thing to do. Never again would I joke about its being 'a beautiful day to die,' as they had joked just before boarding the plane.

Chief Campbell helps us remember these core values which can help us to better understand why it happened. Sometimes, when we find ourselves in trying circumstances we ask ourselves, 'Why do we serve?' I believe we will usually find the answer to be: We serve for love, life, liberty, and the pursuit of happiness and also for duty, God, and Country, our community, our country, our families."

-Michael J. Serabian, Sr., M.B.A. National Cargo Security Council and former faculty member, Johns Hopkins University.

ABOUT THE AUTHOR

Chief Fred Campbell has been in law enforcement for over twenty years. He has worked in all size agencies from a two-man all the way to an agency of three thousand personnel. He has the experience as a police officer, police chief, state law enforcement instructor and correction officer. Currently, Chief Campbell is Director of Training for approximately three thousand correction employees in Arkansas and is Chairperson of the State Interagency Training Council which is responsible for training over thirty thousand state employees. *Mr. Campbell is a regional field training coordinator for the National Institute of Correction in Boulder, Colorado* and was formerly on the Board of Directors for the International Law Enforcement Olympics with thirteen states under his jurisdiction. He is a past regional vice president for the Arkansas Chief of Police Association, executive board member for Butler County, Ohio Chief of Police Association, and Arkansas Municipal Police Officer Association, as well as a former police and fire commissioner for the City of White Hall, Arkansas. Currently, he is *President* of the *At Risk Kids Foundation*, which is based in Washington, DC. Mr. Campbell is also a law enforcement consultant, an expert witness in the use of force and a guest speaker for the University of Arkansas, state police and many other law enforcement agencies. He holds a first degree black belt in judo and has the working knowledge of three other martial arts. He has trained SWAT teams, body guards. *As a nationally acclaimed speaker he has dedicated more than twenty five years of his life enhancing the lives of others, both professionally and personally.* He has more than twenty commendations from life-saving to bravery. In 1988 he was given the prestigious honorary *Arkansas State Police Colonel* award. Chief Campbell has been assigned to protect presidents of the United States, and has been body guard to the rich and famous. *He knows law enforcement.*

INTRODUCTION

For more than twenty years, I have been speaking in conventions, schools, and churches about my experiences in law enforcement. I can always tell by my audience's reaction that, when I get to the stories that I am sharing with you in this book, they seem to listen more intently. Adults sit straighter; kids tell others to be quiet, they stop doodling on the program and no one leaves the room. What is it that makes people interested in these stories?

A lady recently asked me to come to her home so her son could hear the story about drugs from someone who has seen it's terrible effects. Since I cannot come to every home or visit every city, I have hopefully done the next best thing. I have put in writing some of my best stories - the ones that I feel can be of help, encouragement or entertainment to you and your family. All the stories are true - as amazing as some of them may seem. I have changed names, dates, and places of some stories so that those who wish to maintain their privacy may do so.

I have included a **"Roll Call" at the ***beginning of each chapter***. Roll call, in law enforcement, is held at the beginning of each shift by the shift commander. It's purpose is to inform the officers coming on duty what occurred on the previous shift and to pass on important information. That is what I hope to do for you at the beginning of each chapter.

Also included, ***after every story* is a **"Searching for the Lesson".** This is the lesson I learned from these situations and wish to share with you. You may learn something different. I encourage you to search further to discover your own personal lesson.

So, let's get ready to go on patrol. Sometimes we will be in a patrol car and at other times, behind jail or prison walls. The badge, though, will reflect the same excitement, humor, horror, encouragement and more. So, buckle up, put on your gun, shine your badge. Let's see what lessons we can learn and see what it is really like to be a law enforcement officer, as I reflect back with you on my life behind the badge.

LAWSUITS

ROLL CALL

Eighty million lawsuits are filed each year in the USA. That's an average of 152 lawsuits per minute. This year, the odds are greater that you will be in court than in the hospital. For law enforcement officers, the possibility of being sued is even worse. Inmates are twice as likely to file a lawsuit than the average population. I have been sued several times for millions of dollars.

Recently I asked a friend of mine, who is a warden at a maximum security prison, in a northern state, "How many times have you been sued?"

"Over eight hundred times," he said, "just since I have been the warden at the max unit."

There's an old police saying, "It is better to be tried by twelve than carried by six." Though I have not yet been carried by six, being tried by twelve is not much fun either.

**Note: As I was putting the finishing touches on this book, I received a phone call from a colleague of mine, who is a sheriff in the northwest. "Looks like I'm being sued again," he said, " and I need your help as an expert witness in court."

"How much and what for this time?" I asked.

"The inmate wants ten million dollars. We recently built a new jail and he says he doesn't get enough natural light in his new cell."

I guess it just never ends!

THE SEVEN MILLION DOLLAR MAN

"You killed him!" a woman named Ethel Patterson began to scream at me from a jail house lobby. "You killed him! You murdered my husband! I'll get you; I'll sue you for everything you've got." She then fell on her knees and began to weep.

I should have known after my first week on the job that law enforcement was going to be a challenging career. I was already being sued my very first week of employment and accused of murder. I was a correction officer with the local sheriff's department in Ohio, and one night as I reported for work at 11:00 pm, I was told to watch the man in the padded cell.

"He's gone crazy, Fred," the officer I was relieving told me.

"What happened?" I inquired.

"He started eating bugs off the wall upstairs in his cell, then he started eating bugs that weren't there. That's when we got worried and called the doc."

"What did the doctor say?" I asked.

"He said for me to give him two aspirins and the King James Bible and he would see him in the morning. I begged the doctor to come in or send him to the hospital. He told me the hospital wouldn't take him if we sent him and the inmate would be fine until in the morning. That's all he said. Well, I got to go, Fred. Good luck."

I checked on the man in the padded cell every half hour. He would scream at me; then he would tell me to get Ethel, his wife, out of his cell. He was, of course, in the padded cell alone. I told my sergeant that this guy needed help, but the sergeant said there was nothing he could do without the doctor's orders. At around 3:00 am, the man finally went to sleep. He was lying on the floor with his back to the door. I checked on him by looking through a small window and the food tray door. He appeared to be sound asleep. At 6:00 am, I went to feed him breakfast. He refused to get up to eat his meal.

"Come on, man, get up. You snooze, you lose. Get up."

The trustee inmate who was helping me feed the prisoners breakfast said, "Open the door and see if he will get up." I wasn't sure that was a good idea. I was new on the job but as the saying goes, "I might have been born late, but it wasn't last night." "This guy could be faking," I told the trustee inmate. "He could jump up and think that I was Ethel and try to kill me."

"Oh, I hadn't thought of that," the inmate said.

"Yeah, sure," I thought. I asked the sergeant, "What I should do?"

He said, "Wait just a minute and I will go back there with you and we will both go in."

In a few minutes, the sergeant was standing next to me. I had the key to the padded cell and I opened it.

"Hey, get up," I said. The man just lay there.

"Hey, you, get up," the sergeant said.

"I'm getting out of here," the trustee inmate said. And he dropped the breakfast tray and ran.

"Big chicken," I thought. Then, I saw why the trustee inmate was running. He had spotted what I now saw was a pool of blood running into the drain in the middle of the cell. I could see where blood had run out of this inmate's mouth. His head was turned toward the back of the cell. So, when I had checked on him throughout the night, all I could see was the back of his head, and he had appeared to be asleep. I then bent down and touched the inmate who was lying in the floor.

"He's cold, real cold, sergeant." It was later determined that the inmate had been dead about 3 hours.

The family first accused me of murder. They said that I had killed him in the night. They later changed their story to neglect and sued seven of us from both shifts, the city, the county, the doctor and the sheriff for seven million dollars each. In the end, the doctor settled out of court. He got out of the lawsuit. The city and the county were both dropped from the suit. That just left the seven officers and the sheriff. We had to go through a full jury trial. They accused me of hating this man, that I had allowed him to die. They said I should have made the doctor report to the jail. Sure!

During the trial their lawyer accused us of lying on the shift logs. "You never checked on this poor man one time the entire night," the lawyer accused.

The jury finally found us not guilty. They determined the cause of death. The inmate died of D-Ts, delirium tremors. It seemed that he was an alcoholic, which none of us had known about, had gone through withdrawal, and died. I guess it was our fault he was an alcoholic and failed to mention it to any of us, when we did his medical evaluation, upon entering the jail.

"What a way to start a new job," I thought. "I hope I don't ever get sued again." Ha!

SEARCHING FOR THE LESSON

This case taught me how important documentation and writing skills are in this type of work. I had documented every time I checked on the inmate and had also documented that I had told my supervisor of my concern. The shift before me had also documented that they had called the doctor twice, that the doctor had refused to come in and see the inmate, and that they had passed all the information on to my shift. "Gee, Ms. Woodruff (my high school English teacher), I'm sorry for not listening like I should have in your class. I never thought I would need all that junk you were trying to teach me." It could have cost me $7 million dollars.

SWEET LITTLE SIXTEEN

I responded to a call on the corner of Mill St. and Rt. 42. The dispatch was a fight-in-progress call. When I arrived at the scene, I saw Chris Johnson, who was the local drug dealer, leaning up against a light pole. Blood was running from his mouth. I stopped the car, got out and approached Chris.

"What happened here, Chris?" I asked.

"What's it look like, man? I just about got killed. Where were you when I needed you?" Chris began to scream.

"Just calm down, Chris," I said.

"Just calm down, calm down!?" Chris screamed, "Don't tell me to calm down!" Then he threw a punch at me and missed. I grabbed him, put him down on the ground, and started to handcuff him when I saw out of the corner of my eye his three brothers and his sister running at me. One had a 2X4 in his hand. I pulled my gun, kept my knee on Chris' back, and told them to get back.

"Kill this pig," Chris screamed at them. "Kill him." When Chris' clan saw my gun, they took off running, and I went back to try to handcuff Chris. Then all of a sudden, they hit me. Chris' brothers had come back around behind my patrol car and jumped in the middle of my back. I was all alone and my back-up was at least ten minutes away. Out in the county, we don't have the luxury of waiting for back-up like we show in the training videos. One brother grabbed me by the head; the other two grabbed me by the shoulders; and Chris' 16 year old sister began to kick me once, then twice, then three times right in the side. Her brothers were beating me and Chris was still yelling, "Kill the pig."

To this day, I'm not sure how I did it. But some how, right before I was about to pass out, I stood up, threw the three brothers off, found my revolver and pointed it at them. I started to pull the trigger. The only thing that kept me from shooting was that I didn't know which one to shoot first. By then, they all had run off. When my back-up arrived, they checked on me and wanted to know what they should do.

"They are all inside that house. I want them all arrested, especially the girl," I said. "I think she's cracked my rib cage."

When they brought her out of the house, she was going crazy and they had to carry her to the patrol car. I watched as the officer pulled away with her in the back seat. All of a sudden, he stopped the car, got out, and started rubbing the back of his head. She had kicked him in the back of the head while he was driving. They had to bring another car to put her in; it had a cage in it. The cage would prevent her from kicking the officer. When they put her in that car, she then began to beat her head up against the screen.

"Get her out of here," I heard the lieutenant say. "Get her out of here."

One week later, after hiring a slick attorney, she did something that was utterly unbelievable. She filed *criminal assault charges against me* and threatened to sue me if I didn't drop all charges against her.

"Assault her?" I said. "She about broke my ribs. I never even touched her. I couldn't touch her. Her brothers had me down on the ground."

"Well, we're going to sue you for a million dollars," her lawyer said, "and keep those charges against you unless you drop some of the charges against her."

I told her lawyer I would reduce none of the charges against her. "I don't care if you send me to jail and sue me for 20 million dollars." I was so angry. I knew in the end, justice would prevail. And it did, (sort of). All charges were dropped against me. The lawsuit was dismissed and she was found guilty, fined fifty dollars and costs. What a country!

SEARCHING FOR THE LESSON

One of the lessons I learned in this situation was, that if I ever got in trouble, I sure knew which lawyer to hire! I also realized that sometimes, the criminal justice system is just that....criminal. I got teased a lot at work. "I thought you were a black belt in karate," my friends would say. "You let a little sixteen year old, sick girl beat you up."

"Sick girl," I said.

"What do you mean sick?"

Then I remembered that during the trial, the girl's lawyer told the jury that the reason his client kicked the officer in the back of the head when they put her in the patrol car and the reason she kept beating her head up against the screen is because she was having an epileptic seizure that night and couldn't control herself.

JAIL HOUSE LAWYERS

In a recent civil liability class I teach, one of my students said, "Mr. Campbell, I thought inmates lost their rights when they come to prison."

The courts are very careful to watch over the rights of incarcerated people. And, in many cases, rightly so. I tell my law enforcement students, "We, many times, are our own worst enemies. Some officers beat prisoners. They plant evidence, and even torture some inmates. The courts have a hard time trusting us."

I do feel though, that sometimes the courts get a little carried away. Let's take a look at some of my favorite lawsuits filed by inmates in Arkansas and around the country.

■ An Arkansas inmate, calling himself a sports fanatic, complains that as a result of cruel and unusual punishment, he was forced to miss the NFL playoffs especially the games between Miami and San Diego, San Diego and Pittsburgh, and Dallas and San Francisco.

■ Recently, I spoke to one of our inmate school administrators. He told me he was sued several years ago by an inmate who didn't want to get out of bed and attend classes. The inmate said it was his Constitutional Right to be ignorant.

■ A Florida inmate, who had killed five people, sues after lightning knocks out the prison's TV satellite dish and all he could watch was network programs, which he says contain violence, profanity, and other objectionable material.

■ The Mississippi Department of Correction could not believe *this* lawsuit. An inmate sues the department for not receiving a scheduled parole hearing, even though he was out on escape when the hearing was to be held!

■ An Arizona death row inmate, sues correction officials for taking away his Gameboy electronic game. *Well, what do you think about that?*

One of my former students was sued by an inmate who is a jail house lawyer. He asked for $656 million and for it to be paid within thirty days. (See attached law suit.) What had this officer done to be sued for $656 million? The officer gave the man a speeding ticket and then arrested him after he refused to sign the ticket. That's it. No violence. No use of force. Just a speeding ticket.

I was on a flight to Washington, DC, and the man sitting next to me told me he was a lawyer. He said, "I represented an inmate last year who had sued the state on bogus charges just so he could get out of his cell, ride in the state van to go to court and look at the girls."

"Why did you represent him?" I asked.

"Somebody's got to do it," he answered. "And if it's the right kind of federal case, it can pay pretty well."

(NOTICE: THIS ATTACHMENT IS INCLUDED AS THE INMATE WROTE AND SUBMITTED IT TO THE COURTS.)

NOTICE AND DEMAND

Pursuant to Constitutional, Commercial, and Biblical Law

You are hereby notified of the following violations you have committed, whether by omission, negligence, complicity, conspiracy, or contract.

You are hereby ordered to pay to the undersigned or his heirs or assigns the following sums:

FOR THE VIOLATIONS OF THE U.S. CONSTITUTION

Amendment	Number of violations	Amount due
#1	12	$ 120,000
#2	4	$ 40,000
#4	11	$ 110,000
#5	970	$9,700,000 (plus $50,000 per day from date of this notice)
#6	11	$ 110,000
#7	11	$ 110,000
#8	17	$ 170,000
#9	990	$9,900,000 (plus $50,000 per day from date of this notice)
#10	2,026	$20,260,000 (plus $100,000 per day from date of this notice)
Section totals	4,052	$40,520,000 (plus $200,000 per day from date of this notice)

FOR VIOLATIONS OF ARKANSAS CONSTITUTION

Article 11 Section #	Number of violations	Amount due
1	4,052	$40,520,000
2	4,052	$40,520,000
3	4,052	$40,520,000
5	760	$ 7,600,000 (plus $40,000 per day from date of this notice)
7	11	$ 110,000
8	11	$ 110,000
9	16	$ 160,000
10	16	$ 160,000
11	16	$ 160,000
12	4,052	$40,520,000
13	4,052	$40,520,000
15	4,052	$40,520,000
17	17	$ 170,000
18	4,052	$40,520,000
20	4,052	$40,520,000
21	4,052	$40,520,000 (plus $50,000 per day from date of this notice)
22	4,052	$40,520,000 (plus $50,000 per day from date of this notice)
24	4,052	$40,520,000
25	4,052	$40,520,000
26	4,052	$40,520,000
27	4,052	$40,520,000
29	4,052	$40,520,000
Amendment 16	11	$ 110,000
Section totals	61,638	$616,380,000 (plus $140,000per day from date of this notice)
Total amount due and payable:		**$656,900,000 (plus $340,000 per day from date of this notice)**

I,________ do solemnly swear that I will support and defend the organic Constitution of the United States of America against all enemies, foreign and domestic; that I will bear true faith and allegiance to the same; that I take this oath freely, without any mental reservation or purpose of evasion; so help me God.

SEARCHING FOR THE LESSON

Something must be done, not only with the frivolous lawsuits that appear in the criminal justice system but with lawsuits in general. Now it is as important to have legal insurance as medical insurance. Your attorney's phone number could be as important to know as your doctor's. I bet that your doctor knows the phone number of his attorney! Unfortunately, this is the kind of world we now live in.

DRUGS

ROLL CALL

In the last five years, teenage drug abuse has doubled. Cocaine in all forms increased among high school seniors. Daily use of marijuana by high school seniors increased fifty eight percent. Thirty-one percent of high school seniors, twenty five percent of high school sophomores, and fifteen percent of eighth graders admitted to binge drinking according to a news release survey on teen drug abuse.

Drug and alcohol abuse is not just a problem with teenagers. It continues to be a major problem for adults as well. It's been said that eighty percent of our adult prison population have a drug and/or alcohol problem. Ask any law enforcement officer and he or she will be able to tell you story after story like the ones you are about to read.

CHOICES

I was 16 years old when I was offered my first marijuana cigarette. It was the 60's. "Everybody is doing it," Troy said.

Troy Anderson was one of my best friends. He was one of the smartest kids in school. At one time, he had wanted to work at NASA and some day be an astronaut.

As Troy began to inhale his marijuana cigarette, he seemed to be in agony. He kept holding his breath. It looked like he was going to pass out. Then all of a sudden he exhaled and began to laugh. Little did I realize then, that in the next few moments, the destiny of two friends would be sealed. Troy looked at me, laughed and said, "Here, man, take a drag. It will make you high."

I'll never forget looking at Troy and saying, "Man, was that fun? You looked like you were about to die."

"No, man, it's groovy. Here take a drag."

For years, I have thought about my answer to Troy: why I said what I said and what would have happened if I had answered differently. My answer seems so easy now, and to be honest, I don't remember it being so difficult then.

I looked at Troy and simply said, "No, thanks, man."

I remember thinking, "My parents would kill me if they ever found out; my football coach would go nuts." The whole process looked pretty stupid. Troy just smiled and kept on smoking. I guess I was one of the first, "just say no" kids.

After high school, Troy went off to college to begin his studies toward fulfilling his goal of becoming an astronaut. I eventually chose to become a cop.

Some years later, something happened that would remind me of Troy Anderson. It was a cold, late Ohio evening when I got the call. An abandoned vehicle was blocking part of the roadway on a country road. I started to respond but was called off and sent on another call.

Instead, a friend of mine handled the dispatch. Later that evening, he told me what happened.

Mike said he responded to the call and found the abandoned vehicle just as reported. It appeared someone had run off the road, hit the telephone pole and then left the scene. The vehicle was a jeep with no license tags. Just as Mike was about to call a wrecker, he noticed something hanging on the front bumper. It looked like a pair of legs. No, surely not. He hadn't seen any blood that might reveal that someone was injured, but it was very dark out. Maybe he had missed something. Mike told me that as he went around in front of the jeep, he saw what it was. To his surprise, there was a headless man hanging on the front bumper.

"I couldn't believe my eyes," Mike said. "He was just hanging there without a head." What had happened was that the driver had lost control of his jeep and had run over a large rock. Since he didn't have on a seat belt, the jolt threw him through the cloth roof, out in front of the jeep, up against the telephone pole. Then the jeep slammed into him and cut off his head.

"Craziest thing I ever saw," Mike said. "Head just cut off. He was hanging by his neck between the pole and front bumper."

As Mike began to finish his accident report in the roll call room at the end of his shift, he handed me something. "I found this in his front pocket." (It was a vial of cocaine.)

"Did you find any more dope?" I asked Mike.

"No, that's it," he said. "Oh by the way, Fred, I've got this guy's driver's license. I've seen him around. See if you know him."

"What's his name?" I asked.

"Troy," Mike said, "Troy Anderson."

Oh, no. When I looked at the driver's license, I knew it was my friend from high school.

When I went to Troy's funeral, I couldn't help but think back to that day when Troy asked me to take a hit off his marijuana cigarette.

I wondered what would have happened had I said yes. It appears that Troy and I made different choices and took different roads. Mine, so far, has been very rewarding. His road from the beginning was marked.........Dead End. "It looks like you're about to die," I remember telling Troy the day he offered me that marijuana cigarette. Little did I know when I made that statement at sixteen years old that one day I would be asked to identify his headless body from a driver's license photo while working the late shift at the sheriff's office.

"Sleep old friend, sleep tonight. For the life you chose ended tonight. On a lonely, cold, country road, I weep for you and your soul. Too young to die, they said of you, but they knew not the things I knew."

SEARCHING FOR THE LESSON

At Troy's funeral, I learned that his obituary listed his occupation as a chimney sweep. I suppose the dreams that Troy had of working at NASA and the space program had long been forsaken. It appeared that the highest he could get was a roof top - and a cocaine high. What a waste — choose today the master you will serve. "Here man, take a drag, it'll make you high," Troy had told me when I was sixteen years old. In the end it only got *him* six feet under.

SOOEY ... PIG

The local high school called and asked if I would give a talk on drugs and alcohol abuse. It was prom time and they wanted to remind their students about drinking and driving. As I entered the cafeteria, about two hundred students were waiting for my entrance. When the principal introduced me, there were a few boos, but one kid in particular began snorting like a pig. He kept it up so long that the principal had him removed and later made him apologize to me.

"That's Phil Barney," the principal said, "he's nothing but trouble."

"Oh, don't worry," I said. "I'm used to it, besides, some day he may be begging us for help." Little did I know that it would be so soon. On prom night, Phil and one of his buddies got drunk and started knocking over mail boxes by the dozen in Phil's old car. When the police were called, Phil took off at a high rate of speed. What happened next is not clear but eventually Phil was driving so fast and was so drunk that he lost control of his car and flipped it three times before it finally landed upside down, in a ditch. Phil was trapped in the car. The passenger, who was thrown from the car and was unhurt, ran for help. I was not working that night, but the officer who worked the accident told me that when he pulled up on the scene, *Phil was begging for help.*

"I did all I could," the officer said, "but all of a sudden the car caught on fire. Phil began to scream louder and louder, 'please, oh God, please help me, don't let me die.' But the car was so hot that we could not get near it."

Phil died a horrible death inside that car.

One of the amazing things about this story is that it happened almost directly in front of my house. I slept through the whole thing. If I had been awake, I could have been on the scene in a matter of minutes, and perhaps could have pulled Phil from the car. I've often wondered if Phil had stayed and heard my speech if it would have made a difference. Maybe not, but I know his family, friends and a couple of cops who wish it would have.

SEARCHING FOR THE LESSON

I remember a little Sunday School song that says, "Oh, be careful little mouth what you say, oh, be careful little mouth what you say, for the Father up above is looking down in love, so be careful little mouth what you say."

Phil's problem was not only the foot that he put in his mouth the day of my lecture, but the bigger problem was the liquor it was replaced with.

DWF

If drinking and driving don't mix, how about drinking and flying? I'm told that many small airplane crashes are a result of the pilot being drunk.

My first plane crash response occurred early in my career. I was dispatched to the hospital, not to the scene. I was told to help unload the bodies and help with the paper work. When I arrived at the hospital, I met with the coroner who told me what happened.

"Looks like a DWF, Fred," the coroner said.

"DWF?" I asked, "what's that?"

"Drinking while flying. It appears the pilot was drinking and couldn't find the runway. That's him there," he said, "in that body bag. Help me get him inside."

When I picked up the bag, it slushed from one end to the other. "What's in there?" I asked.

"All that's left of the pilot, son. When the plane crashed, it threw him through the windshield into the propeller. Nothing's left but hamburger. That bag over there holds a crispy critter."

"What's that?" I asked.

"That one got trapped in the plane. The plane caught on fire and burnt her up."

"And the other one?" I asked.

"Don't know if it's a man or woman. Found it laying out in the field with no head. Body looks like mush. They still haven't found that head."

I couldn't take it any longer, I ran from the coroner's van to the side of the building to throw up what I thought were my guts.

"Sorry, boy," the coroner said. "I didn't know this was your first plane crash. My fault. Let's get these bodies inside."

It was also my first time to enter the cold refrigerated hospital morgue. There were bodies everywhere. We laid the body bags on the floor since there was no room any where else to place them. Death was everywhere. It brought a reality to my life. Someday I have a reservation for this room. Which corner will I be thrown in?

"Hey, boy!" the coroner yelled at me, awakening me from my mental gaze, "Come on. You want me to lock you in here?"

"Not yet," I said, as I ran for the door at a sprinter's pace.

"Hey, kid," the coroner said, "I'll buy breakfast when we're done."

Needless to say, I had to run back out to the side of the building at the mention of breakfast.

"Rookies," I heard the Coroner say under his breath, "Why do they send me rookies?"

SEARCHING FOR THE LESSON

Planes, trains, and automobiles. Isn't it amazing that we still think we can mix vodka and transportation and expect that the recipe will not result in a Bloody Mary mess? And how about our own lives? We all have a reservation in a cold morgue one day. Young or old, death respects no one. But the reservation at the morgue for the drunk or addict will very likely be an early one.

LIFE IS BUT A VAPOR

ROLL CALL

"Whereas ye know not what shall be on the morrow. For what is your life? It is even a vapor that appeareth for a little time and then vanisheth away." (James 4:14)

As a police officer, I have seen death over and over again. I have seen people hanged, shot, and stabbed, cut in half, shot in two. I have seen murder, suicide, accidental death. One thing I have learned for certain is that death comes to all ages and sizes, regardless of status. The good die along with the bad.

Are you ready for that day? Not only for yourself, but for your loved ones, too? What if today was the last day of your husband's or wife's or child's life? Do they know you love them? Or would you have to tell it to a cold, rigid body lying in a casket? Let's see what we can learn from the next three stories about life and death.

DADDY'S GIRL

US Highway 128 is one of the deadliest highways in the USA. This deadly highway curves like a poisonous snake, just waiting to strike out at it's next victim. It leaves behind a warning for it's future prey, a plethora of white wooden crosses, reaching toward the sky. Bleached by the element of time, the crosses memorialize the countless victims that laid in it's path and fed it's insatiable hunger. I had a feeling that tonight would be another night that #128 would be a road to death - a destination many had traveled before. As I left the roll call room and headed for my patrol car, the crack of thunder echoed throughout the building. "A perfect night to be working upstairs in the jail," I thought. Sometimes I wondered why I had ever asked to be transferred to the patrol division. It didn't take long for the dispatcher to send me on my first accident of the evening. "US Highway 128," she stated. "Approximately 6 miles west of the city limits. Possible injury. Ambulance en route." As I pulled up on the scene, I could tell it was more than a possible injury accident. A small foreign car had run into the rear end of a stalled semi truck. As I jumped out of my patrol car, I could smell that familiar smell of death. As I approached the back of the truck, the paramedic who was already on the scene came to me, and said it was a DOA (dead on arrival). "Her body is pinned in the front seat," he said. "Her head is in the back. Decapitated. Cut her head clean off the body. I've got the truck driver in the ambulance," he said. "He's shaken up but I think he's going to be all right".

I called the dispatcher on my portable radio and told her to send two wreckers. After I had finished taking pictures, the wreckers showed up and began to untangle the mass of steel. As I was about to head back to my patrol car, I heard a scream that cut me to the bone. I quickly turned around and saw Tim, the wrecker driver, on his knees, banging his head and fists on to the side of the small car, which was still stuck under the truck. I couldn't believe he was so upset; he had seen so many wrecks on this deadly highway. I ran to him and asked, "Tim, what's wrong? What's wrong?" He did not respond to my question. "Tim," I said, "we can't get the body out until you can get these two vehicles apart." "What's wrong?" I asked, once more.

As I looked and waited for him to reply, I could see that the sheet that the paramedic had placed over the body parts had blown off the head which was in the back seat. "Oh, my God," he cried, "that's my daughter. That's my baby girl. Oh, God. Oh, God. Oh, my baby. Please do something," he screamed. "Please do something."

But there was nothing anyone could do. As I drove by the scene a week later, I saw a white cross with pink flowers marking the spot of the tragic scene. US Hwy. 128 had claimed yet another victim for its overflowing graveyard. As I was writing this book, I told my wife I was going to add this story to it. "Write it quickly, honey," she said, "so you won't forget even one detail."

I paused for a moment and then said, "Honey, don't worry, unfortunately there are some things you just never forget."

*Footnote: This story is a composite of several officers' memories of the crash scene in a small southern state.

SEARCHING FOR THE LESSON

Death comes to us all. Even the undertaker must decide how he will be buried. The pain of losing your own child must hurt the most. Love them while you have them and make sure they know it. Spend time with them. Help them prepare to meet you when life is over. Then you will have but a short time to be apart.

LAST BREATH

Here's a question. What does a lonely country road, two kids in a Trans Am, and an Amtrak train have in common? The answer is destiny. I had worked all kinds of accidents; car, truck, motorcycle, even a plane crash. But this was my first train wreck. As I pulled up to the scene, I saw that this was a passenger train - not a freight. People were getting off the train and were standing everywhere. Approximately a quarter mile down the track, I saw a twisted car laying along the track. As I began to run toward the car, the hissing air brakes of the train and the screaming of the passengers made the hair rise up on the back of my neck. When I finally got to the wrecked car, I had to order people back into the train. One man, who had gotten off the train to take pictures of this gruesome sight, was throwing up alongside the track. "Good enough for him, " I thought. I peered into the mangled car and saw two young looking boys still trapped in the car. I believed that the two were dead. I reached down to check the pulse of the driver and suddenly he opened his eyes and looked straight at me. As I was getting over this brief shock, the young boy tried to say something. I got very close to his mouth so I could hear what he was trying to say. He opened his mouth one last time and all I could hear was his last gasp of breath. I have often wondered over the years what that young boy was trying to tell me.

What would *you* have said if you knew you were about to die? The chances are that your comments wouldn't have been about the stock market. Do the ones you care about the most know that you love them? Do you tell them so? How often? Don't rely on a cop to pass that information on for you at your time of death. You never know; you might be out of breath.

The following is my poem "Reflection of Gold". The above story is the inspiration for the entire poem.

REFLECTION OF GOLD

A wedding now has taken place,
A golden ring has set the pace.
An Olympic runner has won the race,
A golden medal he has embraced.
A common factor I have with these,
A badge of gold I pin to me.
In the morning as I get dressed,
The mirror reflects it from my chest.

I stand there sometimes and I'm amazed,
And wonder what this badge will bring today.
As the mirror reflects a shining knight,
My mind reflects some fearful nights;
The blue lights flashing all around,
The smell of death I can see them now.
I'm running down the railroad tracks,
A hissing train, an eerie sound.
A car is twisted and torn in half,
Two youths lay dying, they groan their last.
People screaming all around,
I haven't time to mourn them now.
This situation I must control;
That's my job, I'm a cop, you know.
The coroner's come and done his task,
The people gone, the train back on track.
Now I'm alone, the paperwork starts,
But my hands are shaking and my loud beating heart,
And the tears begin to come slowly down.
I quickly look to make sure no one's around,
A crying Trojan must not be found.

The mirror reflects so many things,
The squealing tires the asphalt brings,
A mother cries, her child is dead.
A husband cries as I approach the door,
His wife, a gun, she's tried before.
The blood stains perhaps I will soon forget,
But not the eyes of three-year old Annette.

Sometimes I wonder if it's worth it all,
On those quiet nights when there are few calls.
Some call us pigs, they make their sounds,
The attorney screams "we have no grounds."
The chief, he says he has received a complaint,
City Hall says, they have no money, they're not a bank.

Mirror, mirror, on my wall
Am I the craziest of them all.
A thousand times I've sworn, I've left.
But the badge of gold is still on my chest.
And even at the thought of death,
A gunman's bullet at its best,
Somehow, this job, I love to do,
A cop I am, a man in blue.

So golden shield reflect today,
On a thousand cops who feel this way.
The job we have is strange and unique,
And even though wage is weak.
May you shine on this today,
To a public who's not sure what to say.
That we are cops and we are proud
As we serve them, from behind you,

Our golden shroud.

THE POLICE OFFICER WHO DREW THIS PICTURE FOR MY POEM "REFLECTIONS OF GOLD," WAS SHOT IN THE FACE DURING A HOSTAGE SITUATION AND NEARLY LOST HIS LIFE.

'TIL DEATH DO WE PART

The Chief had ordered all patrol cars to leave the station and to find a place to park. "Don't move unless it is an emergency," he said. In many parts of the US, this would be a strange order for a chief to give his patrol officers, but in Ohio, in January, with ten inches of snow on the ground and temperature below zero, no one was complaining.

At around 2:00 am, I had a feeling that I needed to be somewhere, but I didn't know where. I decided to take a drive down Highway 177. I wasn't going to go far. I felt like it was an emergency. I knew I could take the heat if I didn't travel too far from my assigned area. About one mile down the road, I saw it - a car covered with snow, lying in a ditch. The car looked like it had been there for a long time. The snow plow had been by it several times and had pushed snow up against it. It was not unusual to see a car off in a ditch in such weather as this. I started to drive by and then it hit me that this might be why I had that feeling to drive down the highway. I needed to get out and check the car. As I stepped out of the car, the wind hit me like a jack hammer. I had never felt so cold in my life. "This sure was a dumb idea," I thought. I approached the stranded car and wiped some of the snow off the passenger window and then I saw them - two elderly people cuddled up in each other's arms. "Oh, my God," I thought. "How long have they been in there?" I banged on the window but got no response. I tried to open the door but it was locked. I yelled at the top of my voice; there was no answer. My only thought was to break out a window in the car which is not normally an easy task. But this time, it broke out very quickly. I reached in and unlocked the door, and I saw a very sad but beautiful sight - an older couple in their 70's, I would guess, arms wrapped around each other, hugging each other. They seemed to be at such peace - as if they knew they were never going to be found alive and they were glad they could at least die in each other's arms - sharing each other's warmth. I checked their pulse and could find none; they were cold as ice. I stared at them for a moment, taking in the sad, but touching scene.

In time, the cold wind blowing through the car awakened me from this frozen moment. I started to exit their car to radio for the coroner when all of a sudden the man turned his head toward me and asked, “Son, what time is it?”

I actually slipped on the ice and fell on the roadway in disbelief. “You’re alive,” I shouted.

“Please, son, help my wife, we have been here a long time.”

The ambulance arrived on the scene more quickly than I had expected. I could not leave my area, so an officer closer in to the hospital took the report for me. He later told me that the man’s wife was also alive, and other than some frost bite, they would both be fine.

“I’m sure glad I listened to that small still voice somewhere deep in my soul,” I thought to myself.

“Yeah,” said another voice, “and you better be glad you didn’t wreck the patrol car, too.”

SEARCHING FOR THE LESSON

What would you do if you knew you only had hours to live? What must this couple have been thinking and talking about during their agonizing wait for help? Some possibilities might include their children and grandchildren, reflecting on their lives together as husband and wife. Their eternity and rescue was probably among their predominant thoughts. And perhaps, finally, their comfort came in believing that they could at least share their death experience.

I believe above all, the state in which this couple found themselves, had to bring into perspective that which is really important: their relationships with God and family and friends.

I never saw or heard from this couple again but I will always remember the way in which these two held on to each other at the point of death. "What a way to go," I thought. "What a way to go."

1984 - THE BLOODY BADGES

ROLL CALL

In the 1960's, they called police officers "pigs". In the 1970's, not long after I became an officer, I heard someone say as I walked by in uniform, "I smell bacon." Recently, I was reminded of this again when I heard that a police officer was killed in Denver, Colorado and a dead pig with the officer's name written on it was found lying in the streets.

Over the years, I have buried fifteen of my former police or correction officer students. I have been asked to read my poem, "A Reflection of Gold" at some of their funerals. (This poem appears in this book.) It never gets any easier as the years go by, but there is one year I will never forget - 1984. Not because it was the year George Orwell's book "1984" was to become famous again, but it was because it would be a year of bloodshed for Arkansas police officers. Look behind my badge with me at the death of some of my friends and let's see what we can learn.

IN THE BEGINNING

Saturday, March 31, 1984

It all started on this date. During the early hours of the morning, Miller County Arkansas Deputy Charles Barnes was patrolling a country road. Deputy Barnes' patrol car headlights illuminated what appeared to be a stranded motorist, and two male subjects began flagging the deputy down as if they were in need of help. Later, they admitted that it was not help they were seeking that night at all. Officer Barnes radioed the vehicle's license plate number to the dispatcher and exited his patrol car to lend aid to the stranded motorist. As the officer approached the two individuals, a third subject who was hiding, ambushed the deputy. After radio contact could not be made with Deputy Barnes, back up officers were sent to his location. They found Deputy Barnes lying on the ground beside his marked cruiser. He had been shot twice in the back of the head. A man hunt soon began for the suspects.

One suspect was located later that morning and was killed in an exchange of gun fire. The two additional suspects were later arrested and charged with murder. These two suspects later stated, "All we wanted to do that night was flag someone down and kill them." Deputy Barnes just happened to be that one.

This deranged slaying was the beginning of a killing spree of police officers that seemingly had no end. Arkansas is a small southern state. Though Arkansas has always had its share of violence and police killings, this violence has never been of the magnitude of other larger states. In the year 1983, there was only one officer killed in Arkansas. In 1982, four officers were killed. In 1981 there were three, and in 1980, there were two, but the year 1984 was totally different. This was the first year in Arkansas recorded history that so many officers were slain.

TROOPER DOWN

Saturday, June 30, 1984

Arkansas State Trooper Louis Bryant, age 37, an African American, had pulled over a van at 4:15 pm. The driver was a white male, age 54. Trooper Bryant had called in a driver's license check. While waiting for the information, the driver of the van opened fire on him with a .45 caliber handgun, fatally wounding the officer. Trooper Bryant's wife was, at the moment, driving down the same road with her children and saw her husband lying in the patrol car. She frantically picked up her husband's police radio and called for help. It was too late.

The assailant who had fled the scene was later involved in a shoot-out with officers in Oklahoma. He was shot five times and *lived.* It was later determined that the assailant was a member of the survivalist group, "The Covenant, the Sword and the Arm of the Lord." This group was found to have a camp in northern Arkansas. It was said that the killer hated African Americans so badly, that he was glad to hear Trooper Bryant was dead. It may have been the reason he killed the Trooper. When would all this stop?

NO JOKING MATTER

Tuesday, July 1, 1984

The senseless deaths continued. Officer Ben Wesson, age 21 of Millville, Arkansas, continued what had become a chain of slain police officers. Officer Wesson had gotten off work at around 1:00 am, Tuesday morning. He and several off duty officers had gotten together after work and were visiting with some friends. Then, for no apparent reason, Officer Wesson put a borrowed .38 caliber revolver to his head and pulled the trigger. The weapon discharged and Officer Wesson died about ninety minutes later at a local hospital. There was, of course, a full investigation of the incident. Investigators were unable to turn up very much information. Witnesses stated it all happened so fast; they thought Ben was just kidding around. The police later labeled the shooting as accidental. If Officer Wesson was kidding, none of us were laughing. A fine young 21-year old officer lay dead as the blood of police officers continued to run across Arkansas soil.

DRIVING IN YOUR OWN FUNERAL PROCESSION

Thursday, July 5, 1984

The funeral service for Trooper Louis Bryant was attended by police officers as far away as New Jersey and Florida. Hundreds of local police officers from all over our state, also attended. But on this day, Trooper Bryant's funeral service would be short by four. Captain William Mills, Patrolman William Gilham, Sergeant Roy Brewer, and Patrolman Herman Jones, all from the DeQueen, Arkansas Police Department, were en route in an eleven car police caravan to the funeral services of Trooper Bryant. The four officers were all riding together in one marked police unit. Their chief, Bill Jones, was several cars ahead of the officers and the officers' wives were several cars behind their husbands. Little did these officers know that the funeral caravan they were driving in this day was not Trooper Bryant's, *but their own.* As the police caravan rounded a curve, a subject driving a semi truck, crossed over the center line and struck the four officers' police car head on. The car was crushed under the tires of the huge truck and the caravan came to a halt. The four officers' wives, along with the chief and others, tried to help the four, who were trapped, but the car was so badly crushed, no one could get inside the vehicle. The officers had died instantly. The car had to be removed from the scene to extract the officers' bodies. The driver of the truck, who was *not* badly injured, was arrested and later charged with four counts of manslaughter and DWI.

These four officers were all my personal friends. They had recently been students in our PR 24 Baton Class. I have dined with them and been in some of their homes and met their families. Even as I write these words, and though I have reread the story many times, my soul still grieves for them and their families. Five days after the incident, Captain Mills' wife, Sarah, gave birth to their son, John Quinnis Mills. This was the name her husband wanted to give their child.

FRIDAY THE 13TH

Friday, July 13, 1984

This Friday the 13th would truly be a nightmare for Chief Leonard Cross and Patrolman Roy Leon, Jr., of Cotton Plant, Arkansas, Police Department. The incident occurred around 9:00 pm. That evening, Chief Cross was riding patrol with his new officer, Patrolman Leon. The two officers spotted a suspicious-looking motorcycle driven by a juvenile. The officers ran the license plate number through the computer and it came back that the motorcycle was stolen. After stopping and talking to the juvenile, the officers, along with the juvenile, turned and started to walk toward the patrol car. As they were walking, the juvenile jumped Chief Cross and took the Chief's .357 magnum handgun away from him and shot him in the groin area. The assailant then turned and shot Patrolman Leon through the rib area, killing him instantly. As Patrolman Leon lay dead on the ground, bystanders at the scene stole his collar brass, badge, gun, boot knife, and his payroll check. The juvenile fled the scene and was captured later that morning. Chief Cross crawled back to his patrol car and radioed for help. He died later that night en route to the hospital.

In a matter of two weeks, we had lost seven of our brother officers, making a total of nine. But still, the nightmare continued.

MASSACRE IN HOT SPRINGS

Tuesday, July 24, 1984

An incident occurred on this day that Newsweek magazine would call the "Massacre in Hot Springs." Sergeant Wayne Warwick of the Hot Springs, Arkansas Police Department pulled over a subject in front of the county court house for a traffic violation. Sergeant Warwick approached the vehicle, and as he did, the subject exited the car and approached Warwick. After an exchange of words, a struggle occurred between the two. The driver of the car pulled out a .45 caliber pistol and shot Sergeant Warwick three times, seriously wounding him. Sergeant Warwick, though wounded, returned fire with his .357 revolver, striking the subject. Officer Warwick then fell to the ground.

The driver got back in his car and drove to a local motel bar. He entered the bar and immediately shot and killed the bartender. He then went back outside, got a .12 gauge shotgun from his car, re-entered the bar, and killed the bar owner and two customers. Next, he put the gun to his head and killed himself. One of the driver's friends later stated that one day he had heard him say, "I'm going to get in a gun fight with the police."

Sergeant Warwick later died from the wounds he received in this gun battle.

SEARCHING FOR THE LESSON

Yes, the year 1984 was a year to remember. It was a year of firsts for many people in the United States. For the first time in our country's history, a major political party nominated a woman, Geraldine Ferraro, to be their candidate for the vice-presidency of the United States. The 1984 Olympic Games brought about many firsts for people all around the world. Many athletes won gold medals for their first performance in the games. The United States will never forget, that for the first time, a black man - Raber Johnson - lit the Olympic torch in Los Angeles to start the games. These firsts are all achievements for people, countries and states - accomplishments that will not be forgotten.

I will remember 1984 because of the slaughter of my former friends and colleagues. I learned that racism is still alive whether you're black, white or blue. I learned that training needed to be changed in order for our officers to be better prepared for these situations.

What have you learned from these stories? Hopefully, you can now better appreciate the professions these men and women have chosen. They constantly put their lives on the line for us all. When they pull us over, they don't know whether we're the good guy who is just speeding or the bad guy who just robbed a bank. And remember, when it is dark and dreary and you hear that bump in the night, police officers are the ones you're going to call. Thank God these men and women are there to take the call.

I AM READING MY POEM, "REFLECTION OF GOLD," AT THE STATE CAPITOL IN THE LAW ENFORCEMENT MEMORIAL DAY SERVICE, HONORING OUR OFFICERS THAT WERE KILLED IN THE LINE OF DUTY IN 1984.

TRAINING

ROLL CALL

As the training director for thousands of employees, you can imagine that I might have a bias toward training. Training, though, is not just helpful in law enforcement.

During one of the televised Olympic Games, I saw an interview with a four-time gold medal winner. He stated that he trained every day for the events in which he participated. He felt that if he did not train this way, he would not win. Those of us in law enforcement realize that there are people who daily plan and train *against* us. They may be in prison, or in a survivalist military camp, or perhaps a religious cult, and they are training for that day in which they will meet us, the officer.

Let's take a look at a couple of training stories from my former students and see what we can learn from their experiences that might help you.

It was Benjamin Franklin who said, "By failing to prepare, you are preparing to fail." There is much wisdom in that short statement.

Be prepared. It is better to be prepared and never need it, than to need it and not have it!

POSITIVE SURVIVAL THINKING

As you read in the previous chapter, 1984 was a terrible year for police officers in Arkansas. After the death of so many of our officers, we began to look at our survival training at the Law Enforcement Academy. One statement I began to preach to my cadets was that they needed "the power of positive survival thinking". Just because you are wounded does not mean you will die. Surgeons have told us that whether a person lives or dies, sometimes depends on whether the person *wants* to live. At the last seminar I attended on officer survival, we were told of a person who had been shot with a BB gun. He thought that it was a pellet from a shotgun, and he died. If you get shot and are still alive, there is a good chance that you will live. *Get up* and return fire; *get up*, stop the bleeding; *get up* and call for help. *Get up*. Live! Think positive survival thoughts. I begin by telling my classes that many more officers who get shot or injured live than die. Chief Clarence Kennedy is a perfect example of this positive attitude.

Chief Clarence Kennedy of Palestine, Arkansas, was working for another department when he became involved in a car chase with a subject who had broken into a home. Chief Kennedy finally caught the subject and was behind his patrol car doing a body search when he looked up and saw a car coming straight for him. The Chief pushed his prisoner out of the way of the car and was trying to jump out of the way himself, when the vehicle hit the patrol car, crushing the Chief between the cars from the waist down. The Chief tried to get up on his legs but couldn't, so he *got up* on his elbows, crawled out of the roadway and sought help.

A few years earlier, Chief Kennedy was also involved in a shooting incident. While at the scene of a family disturbance, several subjects jumped the Chief and got him down on the ground. They then took his .357 service revolver and shot him in the head. Chief Kennedy *got up*, recovered his revolver, returned fire, pursued the subjects and then collapsed as back-up officers arrived. After a short period of recovery, Chief Kennedy was back on the streets.

SEARCHING FOR THE LESSON

It has been said that as a rule....the one who has the most information will have the greatest success in life. Thomas Edison trained himself to believe that failure is not final. He believed each of his more than 10,000, *yes, ten thousand*, failed attempts at creating an electrically powered light bulb, was just one step closer to seeing his dream become reality.

"Most people who succeed in the face of seemingly impossible circumstances are people who simply don't know how to quit." Robert Schuller

Let's look at what Chief Kennedy did. Even though his legs were broken and would later require 23 steel pins, he *got up.* Even though he was shot in the head with his own .357 revolver, he *got up*. If your new business idea fails, *get up.* You have got to remember that if you're down, *get up*. Demand that your mind think positive survival thoughts. You react the way you are trained. Training should be a daily ritual. Whether you are in business or law enforcement, daily positive survival training will ensure that you will react properly in any challenging situation.

ROUTINE STOP

If there is one word which I hate to hear police officers use, the word is "routine." I told a cadet class at the Law Enforcement Academy, "Don't *say* the word, don't *think* the word, don't *use* the word." I dramatized this by taking my dictionary into the class room on their graduation day and cutting the word out of my dictionary. "I don't even want the word in my office," I told them. I hope it is a visual aid which they will never forget. A positive survival thinker must think of the negative in order to be able to think of the positive. Let me explain. There is no "routine" burglar alarm call. There is no "routine" prowler call. There is no "routine" domestic call. They all have the potential of becoming dangerous. Think "weapon". Think "cover". Think "approach". Even if you are a twenty-year veteran on your last traffic stop before you retire, think "survival". I told my class that some officer survival opponents say that kind of thinking leads to paranoia and the abuse of power. I'm not saying that every time you pull a car over you need to jump out of your patrol car and go into a karate stance and approach like a Ninja Warrior. I'm not saying you need to pull your weapon out every time you approach a car. What I am saying is to think, "What if?" To quote an old officer survival saying, "We just want you to just be prepared, not paranoid."

At around 4:00 am on the 24th of July, Deputy Ryan spotted three subjects driving a white pickup very slowly down a country road. The deputy believing the driver to be intoxicated attempted to pull the subjects over. Seeing the officer, the driver began to speed up and a chase ensued. One of the occupants of the truck stuck a shotgun out the window and began firing. The shotgun blast blew out the patrol car's passenger front and back windows. The deputy was injured by the flying glass but was not seriously hurt. The suspects fled the scene and were not captured. Deputy Ryan survived. "I kept my head and did as I was trained," he said later. You can see how quickly a "routine" traffic stop can tun into a deadly situation.

SEARCHING FOR THE LESSON

Electricians, salespeople, CEOs and politicians, all should remember that "routine" can be dangerous for them as well. An electrician should always remember that electricity is dangerous if not treated with respect. A salesperson will be more successful when he expects a "yes" from client, even though the "routine" thought would be to expect to hear "no." The CEO must not take his employees and associates for granted and the politician must never give up and accept defeat if he or she loses an election.

The "routine" procedure would have been for Abraham Lincoln to quit long before he ran for President of the United States. Read on.

Consider the career of President Lincoln:

1831-Failed in business

1832-Defeated for legislature

1833-Again failed in business

1834-Elected to legislature

1835-Sweetheart died

1835-Suffered nervous breakdown

1838-Defeated for speaker of the house

1840-Defeated for elector

1843-Defeated for Congress

1846-Elected to Congress

1848-Defeated for Congress

1855-Defeated for Senate

1856-Defeated for Vice President

1858-Defeated for Senate

1860-Elected President

I think you would agree that Mr. Lincoln had no "routine" career. We can all be grateful that he left with us such a shining example from which to learn.

WHO WANTS AN HONEST COP

Survival training is not only about staying alive physically, but also about morally, spiritually, and ethically. I now share with you a sad letter from one of my former students. Please take time to read it carefully. (It has been included in its original form).

Dear Fred:

I have a little story to tell you. Maybe you can use it in class, and others may learn from my misfortune.

It was my day off, but being a "rookie" I was at home listening to my scanner. There had been a stabbing behind a local bar, and the chief and another officer had responded, and apprehended the suspect, complete with the knife that had been used. The suspect was high on drugs and alcohol, so needless to say there was a scuffle to get him handcuffed. The prisoner was brought to the station and processed. At this time I arrived. I thought maybe I could help and wanted to "get in on the action". You see, this is a small department, and sometimes they need all the help they can get.

We don't have a jail here, so the prisoner was to be transported to a nearby county where they have a jail. The chief asked me if I would go with another officer to take this prisoner to jail. Of course, I said yes! All was going well at this time.

The other officer was driving, and I was riding shotgun. Well, as all prisoners get, this one was calling us every name in the book. The other officer suddenly locked up the brakes on the patrol car, nearly sending me through the windshield, and since the prisoner was handcuffed behind his back, he hit at the screen. The driver said something like "big skunk" and laughed about it.

We had gone on a little farther, and the prisoner started making threats to us and our families. There was another screen test, but this time the driver got out and into the back seat with the prisoner. I didn't look. All I heard were the sound of fist on flesh. It finally ended, and we went on our merry way. We hadn't gone much further, when the same threats were started again. This time the driver stopped the car, and told me to wait inside. He got out, and drug scumbag out into the middle of the street, then kicked the prisoner in the groin, which put him down rather suddenly. The officer then got on top of the prisoner and beat the heck out of him. He was then thrown into the car and taken to jail.

O.K. You say "big deal" this guy is a scumbag, he deserved it. No one will ever know about it. How about when this scumbag has to go the hospital with broken ribs? Of course the doctor wants to know what the heck happened to this poor creature. Well of course nobody knows.

We got back to the station, where the other officer tells the chief what happened. Chief makes no comment about it. Well this whole thing bothered me. I thought at first maybe I was too soft to be a cop. Maybe I'd better get the heck out of dodge. But then I thought about what was drilled into me by Fred Campbell, at the Academy. I believe you said something like it was our duty to protect <u>all</u> people, citizens and scumbags alike. How about the code of ethics? How about our oath of office? Don't these mean a thing? Are these just meaningless words we look at once then forget?

Back to the story. This prisoner filed a civil lawsuit, but against the chief and the other officer. I was not named in it. I was told to stick to the story that the car was never stopped, and nothing happened. The mayor asked me for a statement. I told him I needed to talk to the Chief again first. I was told again to stick to the story. I told the mayor "the car was never stopped, nothing happened, that's what I was told to say." I was advised to get a lawyer so I did. I told my lawyer the whole story. He told me not to make any statements to anyone. Then the FBI came down. They wanted a statement. My lawyer talked with him, and the agent advised for us to try and get an immunity order before making a statement. Throughout this whole thing, I have been harassed by the other officer, and the chief. I have been told that if I don't go along with their story that my law career will be finished. No cop in the world would help one that had ratted on another officer. I have been given lectures on loyalty. They have threatened to fire me. They have accused me of accepting bribes from the defendant.

Well, the city has supposedly agreed to pay a settlement and drop all charges against this person, in exchange the lawsuit will be dropped. Now the city is making an investigation, along with the prosecuting attorney. I will have to make a statement to them sooner or later. If I tell the truth, I will cause another officer to lose his job and career. If I lie, I will have tarnished my badge. If I tell the truth and I don't get a grant of immunity, I have left myself open for criminal charges, since I didn't stop the other officer from beating the prisoner. Remember, only civil charges have been filed, from what I understand the criminal charges will follow.

What would you do? Here you are, still fresh from the Academy, the other officer is called "senior officer", and he has beat heck out of a prisoner. Do you look the other way, or try and stop it? If you look the other way, you are just as bad as the scumbag you're taking to jail. After all, what was he going in for? A violent act!! If you try and stop it, the word will get around that you are soft, and not a good cop. No cop wants a reputation of being easy.

If I could do it all over again I would stop the beating before it started. It would have been so easy to reach over and turn up the radio so we would have not heard the threats. I could have said, I can be better than that guy in the back, lets just hurry and get him to jail and be rid of him. After all, when I took this job, I knew that there would be times like this. Sure, I wanted to thump this guy, but I'm better than that, I'll beat him in court. I'll get into his wallet, where it hurts. Hindsight is 20/20.

Well the other officer has a lawyer supplied by the city, and I'll be paying mine out of my pocket for probably the next year or so. All of a sudden I'm the bad guy. Myself and my family are paying for what the other officer did. Sooner or later this small department will find a reason to get rid of me, and there goes all I have worked so hard for. Who wants an honest cop?

Fred, I want to thank you for your training. I promised you I wouldn't tarnish this badge, and I won't. I may lose it, but I love it. Because of this one officer, it will take five years or more for the people of this town to respect cops again, and to forget what this one guy did. Because of him, many people think all cops are bad. It isn't fair is it?

Thanks for being there, it feels better to tell this to someone, who may understand what I'm going through. Tell the new recruits this story if you want. Maybe they will think about it, so if it ever happens to them, they will have some idea of what to do.

SEARCHING FOR THE LESSON

Education is empowerment. Training is important to us all. But one must use what one has learned. The officer who sent this letter to me was fired approximately one month after I received the letter. In Arkansas, we tried to take the negative (death of our police officers or their unethical acts) and turn it into a positive such as better training so we would never have another year like 1984. We also began to spend more time teaching ethics and ways to survive ethically, as well as physically.

There are people who are training *against you* every day. If you're in the business world, it's probably your competition. Who's trying to defeat you? If you're an employee, it may be a fellow employee who is working to get the next promotion ahead of you by attending classes; going to college while you're watching television. Or perhaps, another employee tries to persuade you to steal "just a tiny little item from your company that they won't even miss." If you're a parent, there are people who are trying to get your children - gangs, cults and even some educators. Perhaps some day, you may need that positive survival thinking as you face death yourself. What ever your situation in life, remember, training prepares you for the day when you may have only a short time to react.

STRESS

ROLL CALL

Life, for all of us, is full of pressure and stress. In 1991, Wanda Holloway was under so much internal stress to see her daughter become a cheerleader for her local high school that she tried to have her daughter's competition murdered.

Phil York had lost all his money in a failed business. Shamed by his failure and the stress of unpaid bills, he set his house on fire to collect the insurance money. All seemed to be going fine with the fire until a firemen found a young boy dead in the bath tub of the burned house. It was later determined that Phil's son had skipped school that day and was hiding in the house when his dad set the fire.

What do you do when things don't go your way?

DEATH HOUSE CHILLS

Frank Lanzo had exhausted all his appeals and would die tonight by lethal injection, in a northwestern state prison. Jim Bell was one of my former students and was assigned to his first death squad duty. His job was to walk inmate Lanzo those famous 17 steps from the death cell to the death chamber. "Dead man walking" was his cry (we never really say that but it sounded good in the movie). Officer Bell was so nervous that his palms began to sweat as he reached to unlock the death chamber cell. Inmate Lanzo had made his peace with God and was eating pizza and laughing with his attorney.

The clock struck 9:00 and Warden Reef told inmate Lanzo and the death chamber team that it was time to go. Officer Bell's legs seemed to go limp, but he made the walk and finally got inmate Lanzo tied down to the gurney. As the death chamber team watched, the needle was placed in Lanzo's arm. Officer Bell was now turning white. It appeared he was going to pass out. Then something quite unique was heard . It was coming from inmate Lanzo. Was it cursing? No. Was it a plea for his life? No. What was it that inmate Lanzo was saying? With a slight smile on his face, he looked at Officer Bell and, I suppose, realizing the stress this young officer was under, simply said, "Chill out, Homes. Everything will be all right." And with that inmate Lanzo passed on into eternity.

SEARCHING FOR THE LESSON

How do you handle stress? In the remaining moments of his life, inmate Lanzo, chose to help someone. (More than likely, in Lanzo's case, he didn't normally handle stress quite so admirably). It has been said that you haven't lived a perfect day, until you have helped someone who can never repay you.

Maybe for at least once in his life, Lanzo, had a perfect day. (Of course, you would have to overlook his impending execution in the evaluation of his day).

Let's not be guilty of waiting until it is nearly too late to have a perfect day.

BULL'S EYE

It is unfortunate, but so many times, police officers handle stress by taking their own lives. Officers are more likely to kill themselves than to be killed in the line of duty.

I had a difficult time deciding in which chapter this story should go. Some thought it should go under humor; they were mostly cops. Others thought it should go under stress. I think it is both but it is also sad.

Bob was a hard-nosed detective, always doing everything by the book. That's why, as a senior range master, he never cut anyone any slack. He said that if you can't shoot straight, you shouldn't be a cop.

Bob, like many police officers, was on his third marriage. His wife came home one night and told him she was leaving. She said she had found a man that would spend time with her and make her happy. Bob, I suppose, decided he couldn't live without this third wife, so late that evening, he picked up his revolver - the one with which he had won so many shooting competitions - stuck the gun to his head, pulled the trigger, and believe it or not, *missed!* Bob later got help for his depression and re-entered law enforcement after being fired from his department for the suicide attempt.

One of the lessons of this story is, of course, to get help before you find yourself in Bob's condition. Some of my cop friends also said that being a bad shot ain't all bad, either.

SEARCHING FOR THE LESSON

Suicide is for the selfish. It leaves everyone else to deal with your problems. Try living for others instead of yourself. You may find out that your problems aren't so big after all.

Suicidal psychology can be charted by a triangle with three corners: 1. all alone 2. inactive, 3. indulging in self pity. Change any one of the corners of that "suicide triangle," and you can prevent a very common cause of death.

OLYMPIC DREAMS (OR NIGHTMARES)

I was told over and over again that nobody would show up. Cops wouldn't spend the money and the chiefs and sheriffs would never let them off work to go. Others just laughed. But I had a dream. I was going to bring the Police Olympic Games to my state. Twenty-four other states had police athletic competition; why not Arkansas? I formed a board of dedicated police officers. We spent money we didn't have. We had pre-registered only one person the night before the on-site registration was to begin. I was under so much stress that I couldn't eat or sleep. What if everyone was right and no one came? I would be the laughing stock of Arkansas. How would I pay for all the medals - over two thousand dollars - that we had gotten on credit or the hotel bill and all the equipment we had bought? Then finally the sun began to rise and I made my way to the hotel where the registration booth was located. Hallelujah!! I saw people standing in line to get into the registration room. Over one hundred and fifty cops showed up that week, and by the time I retired from running the games, hundreds of officers were competing every year and many went on to compete around the world.

It seems like a small thing now, but at the time, it was a mountain. I kept asking myself, "How do you get yourself into these situations? Why don't you just sit back, relax, teach your classes and enjoy life? You bring this stress on yourself." The answer that I gave myself was that all stress is not bad and, in the end, this turned out to be well worth the pressure.

SEARCHING FOR THE LESSON

Don't give up on your dreams, just because people laugh at you or say it can't be done or you begin to feel the stress of the task.

Maybe we can learn something about dreams becoming reality by looking at the experience of one of America's most famous Colonels. I am referring to Col. Sanders of Kentucky Fried Chicken fame.

His story goes something like this: At age sixty five, Col. Sanders received his first Social Security check for one hundred and five dollars and he got mad! Knowing he couldn't live on such a meager income, he began searching within himself to find a way to earn more money. The only possible thing he could come up with was his fried chicken recipe. All who had eaten his fried chicken, loved it. Maybe, just maybe, he could sell his chicken recipe to restaurant owners. He could even teach them how to cook it. His recipe would most certainly cause their businesses to grow. Couldn't he expect to be paid a percentage of the fried chicken sales?

He began knocking on doors with his new product idea. Needless to say, as with any innovative action, he was laughed at and made fun of. He did not allow the laughter to deter him. He had a dream. He believed his innovative idea (franchising) would be a "win-win" situation for him and the restaurant owner.

How many times do you think he and his idea were turned down? Fifty times? Two hundred times? Maybe five hundred times? *How about ONE THOUSAND AND NINE times?* That's right! Colonel Sanders approached 1009 restaurant owners with his new idea of the fried chicken franchise, before he ever heard "yes."

How amazing. I don't know about you, but I probably would have given up when I heard the *50th* rejection, or sooner......Could that be why there is only ONE Colonel Harland Sanders?

Governor Clinton's Proclamation Decree naming the Week of June 13 - 18 as Arkansas Police Olympics Week

Attending the proclamation decree naming the week of june 13-18 as Police Olympics Week in Arkansas at the governor's office at the State Capitol June 1988 were Christopher Huddleston, Brinkley Police Chief Fred Campbell, Jacksonville Police Chief Frank Neeley, Governor Bill Clinton, Olympics Executive Director Rex Huddleston, Mike Huddleston and Ken Brown.

Presentation of Plaques

Colonel Tommy Goodwin, Arkansas State Police Director and Brinkley Chief Fred Campbell.

Olympics Executive Directorr Rex Huddleston and Colonel Tommy Goodwin, Director Arkansas State Police.

GOVERNOR BILL CLINTON HONORING THE ARKANSAS POLICE OLYMPIC GAMES BOARD OF DIRECTORS AND ME. AT THE STATEWIDE NEWS CONFERENCE, GOV. CLINTON DECLARED THE SECOND WEEK IN JUNE, ARKANSAS POLICE OLYMPIC WEEK.

BEHIND THE WALLS

I am often asked, " which do you like being the best - a police officer or correction officer?" They both have their pros and *cons* (forgive the pun). Being a police officer was more exciting - the thrill of the chase or guarding the President of the United States of America. Being a correction officer was equally rewarding. As a correction officer, you have time to try to help someone and see his life change as in the story I tell in this book, Death Row Religion. Of the two professions, the most stressful for me was being a correction officer.

Police officers are killed in the line of duty more often than correction officers but the day to day contact with thousands of convicted felons can wear down the toughest cop on the beat. My police officer friends often say, "Fred, they couldn't pay me enough money to work in that prison." And I tell them, "I understand, and they don't pay us enough either."

How would you like to be locked up twelve hours a day with thousands of convicted felons or jail inmates who belong to gangs like the "Crips", "Bloods", "N.A.W.," "Aryans", "Vice-Lords", "MexMafia" or "Outlaws"? Or be locked up with child molesters, rapists, murderers, or some crazy transsexual, homosexual, heterosexual or the insane, cocaine and deranged? Just another day at work for correction officers around the world.

Jim Farley, a correction officer in the south, told me, "it's the things they throw on you that's the worst." For instance, one inmate saved urine for several days and as Jim walked by, threw it in his face. He said, "It went in my mouth, my eyes, everywhere, but that's not the worst thing. It's the defecation that gets to me." One inmate got revenge on a shift supervisor by taking a large amount of laxatives and, after the laxative led to diarrhea, the inmate saved a large cup full and threw it all over the supervisor," Jim said. "And you know, all we could do was write him up for it!!" he added.

Peggy Beale agrees. She told me that she was assigned to hospital security where there was an inmate patient who had AIDS. This inmate had lost control of his bowels and was wearing a diaper. Peggy told me that when she and the nurses entered the inmate patient's room, he had taken his feces and put it all over his face. "He began laughing at us and when I got closer to him, he said, 'Peggy, now I've got something for you.' He had reached in his diaper before we entered the room and was holding a handful of feces. He threw it all over me," she said. "It was all I could do not to throw up. But the nurses were fighting with him and I had to try to help them keep him under control."

Peggy told me about other body fluids that the male inmates try to throw on the female correction officers but I'll stop with the feces and urine.

That's just part of the stress that a correction officer goes through in a day. Would you like to trade jobs? Hey, somebody's got to do it.

SEARCHING FOR THE LESSON

Probably, we all could agree that there are certain duties or aspects of our jobs that we would label "less than desirable." As you can see, correction officers have quite a lot to put up with. It is how you handle these undesirable duties that determines your peace of mind.

Sir Robert Peale, the founder of the "Bobbies" in England stated, "that a man must have perfect control of his temperament, if he is to be a good law enforcement officer." How is your temperament? Surely, most of us do not face the daily situations that a correctional officer faces. Could it be that your work situation isn't that bad, after all?

SERVICE

ROLL CALL

Have you noticed lately that customer service is a thing of the past at so many places of business?

I was at our local super store the other day looking for a throw rug for my office. I asked a young female employee, who was wearing an ID badge indicating that she worked there, if she could help me. She told me that it wasn't her department. I asked for her help again and she said she couldn't do that. I asked if she could find someone to help me, and she said she couldn't leave her area. She said I would have to go up front, (walk about a mile), and ask them for help.

Recently, I was speaking at a leadership seminar in Atlanta. The company sponsoring the seminar booked me in one of the finest hotels in the area. I was amazed that in my three-day stay with this hotel, no one was smiling - not the maids, cooks or anyone. Not even at the check-out did they say, "Have a nice day, come back and stay with us again." Their bad attitudes further reminded me that the food was cold, the bed hard, and I could never get clean towels when I needed them.

Service, and service with a smile, is a thing of the past for some corporations. Is service important with your organization? How about law enforcement? You don't hear much any more about our being public servants.

SMILE, PLEASE

I was teaching traffic law and radar enforcement at the State Law Enforcement Academy several years ago and one day I told my class of young officers this story. The chief had assigned me to run radar on a road that was known for people violating the speed laws. I know the last thing that people want or need is a speeding ticket. For most people, I told my class, this is the only contact they have with law enforcement; so make it as pleasant as possible.

I do my best to treat everyone in the same friendly way, if they will let me. At around 9:00 am, I pulled over a young woman going sixty-five miles per hour in a forty-five mile per hour zone. "Good morning, ma'am," I said with a smile. "I'm sorry to tell you this but you were going sixty-five miles per hour in a forty-five mile per hour zone. I'm out here today running radar because we have had so many accidents on this highway and I would hate to see you or that little one next to you injured in any way." After I had done the paper work, I handed her the ticket and said with a big smile, "Please drive carefully, ma'am. I hate working accidents, even more than writing tickets."

She looked at me, took her ticket and said, "Thank you, officer." Then she stopped, and said "What am I doing? I just thanked you for giving me a ticket. I can't believe I said that."

"Class," I told my students, "if you can get people to thank you after you have given them a ticket, then you have done a good job."

SEARCHING FOR THE LESSON

Isn't it interesting how a little common courtesy can make people forget some of the pain of slow service in a restaurant, lack of assistance in a department store, or even getting a speeding ticket?

When my son, Andy, was 6 or 7 years old, I noticed him standing very straight and cold faced next to me. "What are your doing, son?" I asked.

"Being a cop, Dad," he replied, "You know, cops don't smile very much." What a bad example I must have been. I have tried to change that over the years.

MAY THE FORCE BE WITH YOU

It was my third day on the job as the new police chief. My phone rang and my secretary said, "They're here to see you, chief."

"Who's here?" I asked.

"Them," she said.

As my door swung open, five very distinguished looking black men came into my office. "We are from the NAACP and the black churches in the area. We want to know what you are going to do about it."

"Do about what?" I asked.

"The beating of our black people. Your officers have been abusing us for years."

I told them I knew there were problems in the past; I was hired to change things. I told them that I was already in the process of writing a new Use of Force policy and I wanted to extend to them the courtesy of seeing it. I also told them I wanted to meet with them quarterly and review any complaints they might have but I was going to stand behind my officers one hundred percent, if they were right. I told them I was also starting a ride along program the next month. I wanted them to be the first to ride one entire shift with my officers and fill out an evaluation form at the end of the shift. I told them, "We work for you. This is not my department. It's the city's and you're a part of the city."

In the nearly four years that I was there, I had the best working relationship with the black community than was ever thought possible. Not only were their complaints reduced, but during my entire term, no lawsuits were filed by any citizen charging abuse by any of our officers. I also increased the number of black officers on the force and promoted the first black supervisor in the city's history. In my office hangs several awards, but one of the ones of which I am most proud, comes from the black citizens of Brinkley. It was given to me when I left the department late in 1989. It says, "To Chief Fred Campbell, in appreciation of your dedicated service to the black citizens of our community."

SEARCHING FOR THE LESSON

I have found that in most cases people want to support their local police department and place of employment. We, as administrators, need to remember that we are public servants who offer a public service. Listen to the people in your community and your employees. Listen to both the good and the bad, and then act accordingly. Booker T. Washington has been quoted as saying, "The world cares very little about what one knows: it is what one is able to do that counts."

GOVERNOR BILL CLINTON HONORS THE BRINKLEY, ARKANSAS POLICE DEPARTMENT.

DO UNTO OTHERS

A university in the south had advertised that they were looking for a professor for their criminal justice program. The university was operated by a very large church in the area. My wife and I had already planned a vacation nearby and thought we would stop on Sunday and join the large congregation for worship services.

As we pulled into the parking lot, there were cars everywhere. "This is going to be great," I thought. We parked our car, got out, and headed for the church. It didn't take long for me to realize that something was wrong. We began to pass hundreds of people and no one said a word. We passed by an usher. Nothing was said. We sat in the pew. Nothing was said during the service. Visitors were not made welcome, from the pulpit, by the Pastor or staff. While the pastor was preaching, I saw someone whom I assumed was one of the professors from the college grading papers. I also noticed that the church was only half full. When the pastor said the last "amen", we walked back by hundreds of people. No one said a word, except "excuse me," as they ran out the back door. "I can't believe it," I said to my wife, "not one person said hello. Glad you're here. No one. Nobody." "Why would anybody want to come to this church or college?" I thought. The church could have been full to overflowing if they had been just a *little* friendly.

I have often been told that your life is the only Bible many people will ever read. How would people classify your life at work, home, school or church if they sat down one night to read it? Would it be classified as fiction or non-fiction? You're the author.

SEARCHING FOR THE LESSON

I once read that Ghandi was asked why he wasn't a Christian. "I think I would have *been* a Christian," he said, "if I would have ever *seen* a Christian." What do people see in you? Do they see things that make them want to join your church, patronize your place of business, or just be your friend? The difference between ordinary and extraordinary is that little "extra." You might be surprised to see what rewards a smile and kind word can bring the giver *and* the receiver.

DEATH ROW RELIGION

Chris Masters was an evil man. He had been sentenced to die in the electric chair for the murder of eighty year old Maude Anderson. Chris entered the home of Miss Anderson late one night and dragged her from her bed, took an ax and drove it through her skull. Then, with the ax still sticking in her head, as she lay dying, he dragged her back into the bedroom and sexually assaulted her. I had seen the crime scene pictures and it was gruesome. Chris was sent to my section of the jail. This section was the isolation area and was where we held death row inmates. He was waiting to be transferred to the state prison for later execution.

I was working the late shift, "11 to 7", so when I first saw him he was asleep in his cell. When he arose that morning for breakfast, he had the look of an evil man - wild looking eyes, hair a mess, and smelled as if he hadn't bathed in a week. I instantly disliked him. I knew too much about the crime which is not always good for a jailer. I remembered my training. "Treat everyone the same," my instructor had said. "Rapists and robbers, treat them all firm, but fair." I couldn't help but think about what Masters had done to old Miss Anderson. Those crime scene pictures haunted me.

"Good morning," Masters said to me.

"Yeah, good morning. How are you doing?" I asked.

"Not bad, for a dead man. How are you doing."

"Okay," I said, "see you later." And with that I was out of there. "I would like to be the one to pull the switch on you," I said to myself, "I'll be glad when you're gone."

I was told that Masters would be with us about thirty days before he would be transferred to the state prison. In those thirty days, something terrible happened. Inmate Masters began to like me. He would wait up so he could talk to me when I came on shift. He said that everybody else made fun of him. One officer in particular taunted him about frying in the electric chair and had given him a headpiece shaped like the one used in the electric chair saying, " you're going to fry, baby."

I was not pleased that he liked me, but I had always tried to treat everyone the same. I was not about to let him change my way of being a correction officer.

Three days before his transfer, something unbelievable happened. It was early one Sunday morning and I was making my final rounds before breakfast. Inmate Masters was up staring at the television, and as I walked by, he looked at me and said, "Officer Campbell, you're a Christian, aren't you?"

I was stunned. "Yeah, Masters, why do you ask?" I certainly didn't think I had displayed any outstanding Christian traits toward him.

"The way you act," he said. "Officer Campbell, do you believe what that man is saying on the TV?"

I looked at the television and saw that he was watching a program called "The Old Time Gospel Hour." "Yes, Masters, I do. I know that man and I believe what he is saying is true. Christ can forgive your sin no matter what's been done."

"Officer Campbell, if I do what that man says, will I go to Heaven?"

What I'm about to tell you may shock some of my Christian brethren. But would you believe that I wasn't sure I wanted that man to go to Heaven? The crime scene pictures began to shoot through my head. The rape and torture of Miss Anderson were still fresh on my mind. Hell is where I wanted him to go. I know that's not the way to think but I won't lie to you. I was still ready to pull the switch on him myself. I looked at him and big tears were in his eyes. "Yeah, Masters," I said gruffly, "do what he says and you can go to Heaven." I left on that note, having done what I thought was above and beyond my Christian duty, and then asked someone else to feed him for me at breakfast. "I'm glad he's just got two more days here," I said to myself, "and then it's off to the electric chair for him. I hate this *jail house religion* so they can look good for a pardon later down the road."

Two Days Left

"Two days left," I thought, when I went to work that next evening. "Two days and he'll be gone." As I made my first rounds that evening, Masters was waiting for me.

"Hey, Officer Campbell, I did what you said yesterday. I prayed and God forgave me of all my sins. I'm trusting Christ to take me to Heaven when I die."

"That's great, Masters," I tried to say with a smile. "That's great."

"Officer Campbell, now I need to get baptized, don't I?"

"Yes, you sure do."

"Well," he said, "I talked to the chaplain today and he said there was no where to baptize me. The sheriff would not let me go to a church and be baptized and the chaplain wouldn't do it where I asked him to."

"Where did you ask him to baptize you, Masters?"

"Upstairs," he said, "upstairs in the old matron quarters. There's a bath tub up there."

I asked myself, "How did he know that there was a bath tub upstairs?" "Oh, well," I said to Masters. "Just wait 'til you get to the state pen, maybe they will baptize you there."

"No," he said, "I don't think I will live that long, Officer Campbell. Will you please do me a favor and baptize me upstairs in the bathtub?"

"What?" I said in disbelief, "Masters, are you crazy? I can't baptize you. I'm not the chaplain."

"I know you're not," he said, "But you're a Christian and I know you have baptized people at the church you go to."

"How'd he know that?" I thought. As I looked at him, he once again began to cry. "Yeah," I thought, "I'm starting to feel sorry for you, but I wonder if you felt sorry for Miss Anderson when she was screaming and begging you for her life?"

"Oh, okay," I said reluctantly, "if you can talk the warden into it, I'll do it."

"Thanks," he said, "Brother, thanks."

I knew I was safe. Warden Pierce would never go for it. He even told me when he hired me, "Boy, he said, "I know you go to church. Don't be trying to convert these people back here. You ain't the Chaplain."

So I went home thinking, "Only one more day with inmate Masters."

One Day Left

I got to work early the next night and when I arrived, there was a note in my employee mail box directing me to see Captain Henderson as soon as I got there. "Hey, Captain," I said, as I knocked on his door.

"I have a note here from the Warden," the Captain said, "it says when you arrive, to get inmate Masters upstairs with a full security detail to the matron quarters and you are to baptize him."

"What?" I said, "Are you kidding? He approved that maniac's request?"

"I guess he did," Captain Henderson said. "They're up there now waiting on you, preacher boy," he said with a sarcastic laugh. As I started to leave he said, "Hey, kid, when you get him under the water, hold him there. You'll be doing us all a favor." And then he roared with laughter.

I headed for the elevator and thought, "You know, that's not a bad idea. Just hold him under."

I stepped off the elevator on to the third floor lobby, feeling like a fool. Here I was, trying to be a professional correction officer, and I'm baptizing some murdering rapist. I knew all the staff were laughing at me. I'm sure they felt like I had been suckered in by this fool. I had gotten caught up in this "little inmate game" he was playing. I then walked into the matron quarters and was escorted back to the bathroom area. Inmate Masters had on a new pair of jail clothes and was standing up in the bath tub which was full of water. The SWAT team commander was standing next to me and said, "Fred, whenever you're ready, go ahead."

Masters was in leg irons and chains. No one trusted him, including me.

"Hey, Masters," I said, "Just sit down in the water and I will pray, say a few words and then I will baptize you." As Chris Masters sat down, I said the same things I had said before at church, "Everyone bow your head and close your eyes for a word of prayer." Then it hit me! "No, no," I shouted, "Keep your eyes open. Heads up." What was I thinking; I didn't want the SWAT team to close their eyes. "Never mind the prayer," I said. I looked at Chris and said, "Chris Masters, upon your public profession of faith in Jesus Christ, I now baptize you, my ('oh, no,' I thought, 'I forgot about this part,) brother, in the name of the Father, Son, and Holy Ghost." And with that said, I pushed him under the water. For a second, I thought about what Captain Henderson had said, but I let him up out of the water.

As his head came up out of the water, he shouted, "Hallelujah! Hallelujah!"

"Yeah, hallelujah," I thought.

Chris thanked me over and over. I could tell he wanted to hug me but he had on too many chains and handcuffs.

"That's okay," I thought. I didn't want him to hug me in front of all these SWAT team guys anyway. I will admit, though, that for the first time I thought that maybe, just maybe, he meant what he was doing and was truly sincere. It didn't matter to me though, because this was it. Masters would be gone tomorrow, but even if he wasn't gone, I was off for the next two days and when I returned I would be on the day shift. All I had to put up with now was the ribbing I would be getting from everybody on my shift.

Overtime

On my first day off, I got a call from Captain Henderson. "Fred, can you come in to work tonight? I know it's your day off but we are really short handed."

"Okay, Captain," I said, "if you really need me, I'll be there."

At roll call meeting that night, Officer Hill told me that the inmate in Cell C-9 was given some medication from the doctor that evening. "The inmate was really nervous," the officer told me, "I guess it's because they are shipping him to death row at the state pen in the morning."

"Who's the inmate?" I asked with a sick feeling in my stomach.

"Inmate Chris Masters," the officer told me.

"Masters," I questioned, "I thought they shipped him yesterday?"

"I guess not," the officer said. "I just gave him his last medication before I came down here to tell you at roll call meeting."

On my first round for the evening, my silent prayers were answered. Inmate Masters was sleeping like a baby. "Good!" I thought, "Maybe he will sleep all night and I won't have to speak to him 'til in the morning." Unfortunately, that was not the case. Little did I know, but my life might soon be over.

"1:00 am, security round - everything okay," my security log would read. 2:00 am. Same entry. But I almost didn't get to write the 3:00 am log entry. As I walked down the cat walk which led me by each prisoner's cell, I couldn't help but think about how hot it was tonight (in those days, there was no air conditioned building for inmates). The smell of sweating bodies hung in the air. The humming of the electric fans had an almost hypnotic effect on me. Then it happened. All appeared to be fine as I walked by Inmate Master's cell. I turned the corner and heard what sounded like an explosion. It threw me back against the wall and then I saw him. Inmate Masters was standing out on the cat walk, looking straight at me. The explosion I had heard was his huge steel cell door crashing up against the concrete wall. He had somehow gotten his cell door open and was escaping. He screamed at the top of his lungs, "I'm going to kill you, man. I'm going to kill you."

"Masters!" I screamed at the top of my voice, "What are you doing?"

Inmate Masters looked at me very closely and said, "Brother Campbell, is that you?"

"Yeah, Masters," I said. "What are you doing?" (For some reason, I didn't mind him calling me 'Brother' this time.)

Then he began to cry. "I didn't think you were working tonight. Thank God, you are here. When that officer on the last shift gave me the medication, he forgot to lock the cell door. Brother Campbell, the devil has been talking to me all night - just like he did the night I killed Miss Anderson. He's been saying, 'Kill that guard. Escape, you fool, escape. Kill that guard and escape.' Thank God, it's you." (At that moment, I was not as thankful to God as he was that I was there.) Then I realized what he meant. "Hurry, Brother Campbell," he said, "go get the keys and lock me in here. God doesn't want me to escape. I can't kill you. You showed me God. Please hurry and get the key."

"Masters," I said, "get back in your cell and lie down. I will go get the key. Just go lie down." Inmate Masters turned around and went back into his cell. I did the fastest thirty yard dash to the key box in recorded jail history. I should have called for help, but I didn't. I grabbed the key, went back to the cell, looked in, and there Inmate Masters was, lying in his bed sound asleep. I locked the cell door, went downstairs and fell exhausted into the office chair.

"What's wrong with you, son?" my sergeant said.

"I'll tell you later, sergeant. Right now, I'm just glad I'm a Christian."

"What?" my sergeant said.

"Nothing, Sarge," I said, "nothing."

Inmate Chris Masters slept in that morning at breakfast. He was shipped to the state pen later that day and put on death row. I have never heard from him again. Later, I was told that he was tried for three murders in another state. He was found guilty of those three murders and sentenced to die in that state's electric chair as well.

SEARCHING FOR THE LESSON

Chris Masters was a mass murderer. If I used his real name, some of you would recognize him. He was truly an evil man. I have learned many things from dealing with him. One is, I'm probably here today writing this because, at least outwardly, I did not judge him. He had already been before a judge. I tried to treat him as I did all other inmates, firm but fair. I listened to him when others wouldn't. I helped him, within proper channels, when asked. Was my heart in it? Not always. But I was bound by a sense of duty and <u>service</u> to God and my profession. We all meet people, whether in the business world or personal life, who we don't like. That's when the test of professionalism in the business world or faith in God comes to light.

It is not always easy being a professional or a Christian. Sometimes you must act out of duty because your heart is simply not in it. I suppose the Golden Rule says it all. "Do unto others, as you would have them do unto you." Not as they would do unto you. Chris Masters killed many people. The key word is "you", as "you" would have them do unto "you". You never know. It just might save your life.

GUARDING THE STARS

ROLL CALL

One of the most interesting times for me was when I began to work with the Secret Service in protecting the President of the United States of America. The amount of work that goes into protecting the president and vice-president is staggering. Once I asked a Secret Service agent if his job was to jump in front of a bullet to save the president's life. He answered, "A dead agent does the president no good. My job is to, hopefully, keep that from happening or at least to get the president out of the way of the bullet." I asked no further questions. I'm sure it was something he had been asked a thousand times before - just as I'm often asked, "Have you ever killed anybody?" I've helped protect two Presidents of the United States of America, several governors, and a host of others. I owe most of what I know about the personal protection business to the Secret Service. Come with me on my first experience in protecting the Vice-President of the United States of America in the story called the "VP and Me."

THE VP AND ME

The Secret Service talked to all of us at roll call meeting. "We want you to know that the Vice President of the United States has just received a death threat. It happens all the time. But you should know that you have a serious job to do. Your job is to watch the crowd, not to become a part of it. Don't shake his hand. Don't ask for an autograph. You're here to work, not play. We will now give you your assignment, Officer Campbell."

"Yes sir," I said.

"You will be assigned to watch the vice president's limo while he is making his speech. Don't let any one near it. You'll be close to Mr. Bush. Keep him safe." I will never forget what happened next.

Vice President Bush was to be the speaker at graduation services at Miami University in Oxford, Ohio. Secret Service agents were everywhere. Bomb sniffing dogs were sniffing away; snipers were placed on top of buildings. I was assigned to guard the back door of the building that the vice-president would use while attending a luncheon early in the day and was also assigned to guard his limo. As the limo pulled up to the back of the building, people started coming from everywhere to see the vice-president. As the vice-president stepped out of the car, he walked over and began shaking hands with the many guests that had been waiting for him. Then he headed straight for me. As he got closer I began to get nervous. It looked like he was coming to talk to me. Then he stopped right in front of me and stuck out his hand. "Oh, no," I thought. "What should I do? They told us not to shake his hand. What if this is a test of the CIA or Secret Service? Maybe this is a fake vice-president and they're just seeing if I can obey orders. But what if this is the real vice-president - I can't be so rude." Then he said something that made me too weak to take the pressure. He said my name.

"Fred," he said. "I just wanted you to know how much I appreciate your being here today to protect Barbara and me. I know it can be a big hassle for you all." Well, that did it. They would just have to lock me up!

"Thank you, Mr. Vice-President," I said as I shook his hand strongly. "Thanks for coming here today." As he left to enter the building, I looked at the Secret Service agent next to me. "Sorry," I said, with a sheepish smile. "Are you going to fire me?"

"No," he said, "you did fine."

"Hey," I said to the agent, "he knew my name. Did you tell him who I was, or did he ask who was that professional-looking officer over there?"

"No," the agent said. "He read the name tag on your uniform."

"Oh, I forgot about that," I said with my ego slightly deflated. I finished the day off without any further tests from the CIA.

Of all the people I have protected, Mr. Bush seems to be a man of high integrity and over all a nice man. I wish I knew him better.

SEARCHING FOR THE LESSON

Abraham Lincoln said, "Nearly all men can stand adversity, but if you want to test a man's character give him power."

One of the greatest problems in America is that we have lost our *attitude of gratitude*. One who possesses this attribute can not be depressed or unhappy. Mr. Bush was under no obligation to thank me for my services. Security is an expected aspect of his position.

From all the Secret Service people I know, never once has any of them made a bad remark about President or Mrs. Bush.

It was an honor to protect such a good man.

DRIVING MISS DAISY

Miss Daisy Bates, the famous civil rights leader who helped desegregate Little Rock Central High School, and a friend of Martin Luther King, was celebrating her eightieth birthday. Thousands would be coming from all over the country - Miss Rosa Parks from Detroit, Stevie Wonder, and possibly the President of the United States of America, Bill Clinton.

I received a call that Miss Bates wanted me to head up a security team for this event. It seems Miss Bates had received a letter stating it was time for this "nigger lady to die."

I was, of course, honored to be asked and immediately accepted the job. When I read the letter that had been sent to Miss Bates, I couldn't believe there were people who still hated this lady. I knew that the president might be coming, so I gave the letter to my friends at the Secret Service for further investigation.

The limo arrived for Miss Bates and the driver drove us to the event. I couldn't help but to apologize for the letter sent to her from, I assume, some one of my race. "Oh, Fred," she said, "don't worry about that, they haven't shot my windows out at my house in a long time." I couldn't explain to her how I felt. She and Miss Rosa Parks were such sweet ladies. I felt so bad for all the wrongs that had been done to them.

"Miss Bates," I said, "I can't do anything about the past, but tonight, this white boy will give his life for you if needed."

"Oh, honey," she said, "let's hope that's not necessary," and she leaned over and kissed me on the cheek.

"Happy Birthday, Miss Bates," I said. Thank God everything went just fine.

SEARCHING FOR THE LESSON

I can't understood why someone would hate a person based on the color of one's skin. Hate crime - yes; hate sin - sure; hate injustice - of course; hate a color - I just don't get it. Perhaps I have my mother to thank for that. Thanks, Mom, because of your upbringing, I just don't get it.

AT THE AIRPORT, GUARDING MISS BATES AND STEVIE WONDER, JUST HOURS BEFORE HER BIRTHDAY CELEBRATION AT THE ARKANSAS STATE HOUSE CONVENTION CENTER.

ESCORTING ROSA PARKS AT THE ARKANSAS GOVERNOR'S MANSION.

ROCK AND ROLL AND WIN

I received a call from the chief of security of one of the richest men in the country. "Mr. Rockefeller has heard about you," the caller said, "and would like me to attend the special weapons class and self defense training you are presenting to the local police department next week. Would it be all right?"

"I would be honored," I told the caller, "but be advised - come prepared to work; it might get a little rough." As the class was about to begin, I noticed two men who did not have on police sweat suits walk into the back of the gym. They approached me and the tall one stuck out his hand and said, "Hello, Fred. I'm Jim Duncan, chief of security for Win Rockefeller."

"Glad to meet you, Jim. Who is this fellow you brought with you, your body guard?"

"No," Jim said with a smile. "This is Mr. Winthrop Rockefeller, my boss. He would like to attend the class along with me. Would that be okay?"

I was so surprised I said nothing for a few seconds. I guess Mr. Rockefeller thought I wasn't going to let him in the class. He said, "Fred, don't worry. I won't hurt you."

We both laughed and I said, "Sure, Mr. Rockefeller, you may join the class, but I won't let these men and women go easy on you. No pain, no gain."

"Thanks, Fred, but please call me Win."

So, with that, the class began. For the next two days, Mr. Rockefeller got hit, thrown and kicked, and did so, in return, just like everyone else. At lunch time the first day, everyone went to McDonald's. My cop friends, not ones to let a free lunch go by, had talked Mr. Rockefeller into buying lunch. When I found out, I said, "No, Mr. Rockefeller, today you are just one of the students."

"You're the boss," he said, "but you tell them. I've got to make it out of town tonight." On the last day of the class, after graduation, we all went to the home of one of the officers for snacks. Mr. Rockefeller and his chief of security also came along and we all had a nice time of fellowship. What a joy he and his security chief were to teach.

As he and his security chief pulled out of the drive way of the officer's home, I thought what a shame this good man needs a security staff. "It's a sign of the times," I thought, "but then, I guess it's always been that way."

SEARCHING FOR THE LESSON

I suppose the lesson I learned those two days is that many times the rich and famous get a bad rap. I have worked around several of them and though they are not perfect, they are flesh and blood, just like the rest of us. Mr. Rockefeller was one of the nicest down-to-earth men I have ever met. He made us all feel at ease; but he was also tough. I told him that he had the heart of a cop. If I could choose someone to be my partner in a patrol car, someone I could trust with my life and be my back-up, he would be one of the few I would choose.

ETHICS

ROLL CALL

How many times have you read about a president of one corporation indicted on theft charges or a CEO of another corporation caught bribing local politicians? I recently read where a high school principal was fired for *stealing toilet paper* from his high school supply room.

Corruption is not just for CEO's or politicians. We all face temptation in our lives and careers.

Let's go behind my badge and meet some officers of the court and see how they handled the temptation that faced them while serving to uphold the law.

THE DARK SIDE OF THE POLICE FORCE

When we think of corruption or a tarnished badge, many times we think of Chicago or New York City, but let's be honest, it's happening everywhere. It seems like you can pick up the paper and read about it every day. While reading the newspaper the other day, I came across these two stories on the same page:

> "GOING TO PRISON - A former captain with the county sheriff's office reported to Circuit Judge John Smith on Monday to begin serving a three-year prison term. He was convicted of conspiracy to commit burglary and theft in connection with a 'sting' operation which he had set up to catch criminals. He was fined $10,000 in addition to the sentence. As a former detective in the criminal investigation division, he was convicted in federal court on a weapons charge." He served 60 days, was placed on three years probation and was fined $1,000.

> "FORMER OFFICER ORDERED TO REPAY $460 IN FINES - A former police sergeant charged with stealing parking ticket fines, was fined $500, ordered to repay $460 and was given a suspended sentence of a year in jail Monday by Municipal Judge Allan Mack. A 26-year veteran, he has until April 24 to make the $460 repayment to the city and has until June 24 to pay the $500 fine and court costs. Judge Mack merged 13 misdemeanor charges of theft of property against the officer. The maximum penalty on each count of theft of property is up to a year in jail and a $1,000 fine."

Did you read the last story closely? A *26 year* veteran was charged with stealing $460. That officer just destroyed a 26-year career for $460! What causes an officer to do this? What does the Code of Ethics have to say about an officer's action?

LAW ENFORCEMENT CODE OF ETHICS

As a Law Enforcement Officer, my fundamental duty is to serve mankind, to safeguard lives and property, to protect the innocent against deception, the weak against oppression or intimidation, and the peaceful against violence or disorder, and to respect the constitutional rights of all men to liberty, equality and justice.

I will keep my private life unsullied as an example to all, maintain courageous and calm in the face of danger, scorn, or ridicule, develop self-restraint, and be constantly mindful of the welfare of others. I will be honest in thought and deed in both my personal and official life; I will be exemplary in obeying the laws of the land and the regulations of my department; and anything I see or hear of a confidential nature or that is confided to me in my official capacity will be kept ever secret unless revelation is necessary in the performance of my duty.

I will never act officiously or permit personal feelings, prejudices, animosities or friendships to influence my decisions. With no compromise for crime and with relentless prosecution of criminals, I will enforce the law courteously and appropriately without fear or favor, malice or ill will, never employing unnecessary force or violence and never accepting gratuities. I recognize the badge of my office as a symbol of public faith, and I accept it as a public trust to be held so long as I am true to the ethics of the police service. I will constantly strive to achieve these objectives and ideals, dedicating myself before God to my chosen profession . . . law enforcement.

SEARCHING FOR THE LESSON

For more than twenty years now, I have seen officers come and go. I have seen them sworn into office by the Code of Ethics, and then, I have seen them swear at it as they leave. What is it about this Code that seems to destroy so many careers?

THE WEBB PAGES

I have met several famous, or infamous, prisoners. Today, one of the most famous of all I have met would be visiting me. As my secretary brought him into my office, I could not help but think, "Here is a man who was the closest friend to the most powerful person in the world - the President of the United States of America - a former chief justice, associate attorney general and a former mayor of a large city in the USA, and now, this large man walks in my office with this small US Marshall behind him." I wondered to myself, "How could this have happened to such a powerful and once respected man?"

"This is Webb Hubbell," the Marshall said. "He is here by court order to speak to your graduating class of correction officers." Mr. Hubbell was a close friend of the President of the United States. He pled guilty to mail fraud and tax evasion and did time in a federal penitentiary. I found Mr. Hubbell to be a very sincere and humble man. He pled guilty and blames only himself. In fact, I told him once, that he was likely the *only guilty man* I could find in prison. Mr. Hubbell, though, said one thing to me that day that I would like to pass on to you. "Corruption starts small. I started taking just a little money from my firm. I always knew I would pay it back. But it had become too much to pay back and I was caught in my own trap. I have betrayed myself, my family, my friends and the President of the USA. If I could only undo all the wrong . . ." Mr. Hubbell then addressed the class.

Dressed in a gray suit, he told the graduates in a 45-minute speech that during his career he was seduced by corruption and gave in to it. He said that in their jobs, the officers must refuse to get drugs for inmates and avoid taking bribes. "He told us how he had made mistakes," Officer Blair, a graduating officer said. "I believe we will think about what he said and remember it when we're faced with difficult situations."

Isn't it interesting how someone can rise so high and so quickly sink to the bottom?

He also told the class what it was like to be in prison. At one time, he was the Chief Justice of the Arkansas Supreme Court and Associate Attorney General of the United States of America! He had gone from putting criminals in prison to being in prison, himself. Daily, he mopped floors and cleaned toilets. As he recalled his first night in prison, he remembered an inmate yelling, "We're gonna get you, Hubbell!" Another screamed, "Don't bother to put your underwear on tonight."

I was afraid for my life," Hubbell told the class, "and that's exactly how it will be for you, if you violate your oath of office and follow in my path."

SEARCHING FOR THE LESSON

As leaders, whether in our home, in business or in law enforcement, we must not only watch the traps set by our competition or enemies, but we must also watch those set by our own minds when we are tired, lonely or desperate.

The king cried, "Who is the enemy in my camp? Who betrays me?"

The prophet cries, "I have him, sir."

"Bring him to me," the king yells. "It will be off with his head."

The prophet said, "He is already here, sir. For the enemy is you."

WEBB HUBBELL EXITING THE CORRECTION ACADEMY, AFTER DELIVERING HIS COURT ORDERED SPEECH TO ACADEMY GRADUATES.

TROOPERS AREN'T FOR SALE

A friend of mine works for a law enforcement agency in Florida. He patrolled part of the Everglades. He told me that at one time he was offered $200,000 just to turn his head when he heard a plane start to land in his patrol sector. That's all - just turn his head and let them land - undisturbed. What's your price? Do you have one?

Late one night, I received a call from my dispatcher. "Chief, Chief," she cried, "Come quick to your office. I have never seen so much money." When I got to the police station, I was told that I was needed in the detective's office. When I opened the door, I saw a suitcase full of money.

My detective looked at me and said, "Chief, so far we have over a half a million dollars. What do you think?"

"I think you better keep counting. And get it all on video."

"Chief," a big tall trooper said from another office, "I pulled him over for speeding on the interstate a little while ago. He said I could have all that money if I would just let him go."

"What did you tell him?" I asked.

"I told him troopers aren't for sale."

Are you for sale? What's your price?

When I spoke to the suspect that the trooper brought in that night, he made me the same offer. "And more. I can get you twice that much," the man said to me. "None of these other cops will ever know about it. Come on, Chief."

"You can be rich. Yeah, rich," I thought, "The richest cop in prison." The man claimed the money wasn't his. He posted bond and I never saw him again. The state confiscated the money and eventually it was divided up between the city, state, and county and was used to buy new police equipment.

SEARCHING FOR THE LESSON

For most officers, it's not a million dollars in cash for which they lose their jobs or go to jail; it's a fifty dollar handgun from the evidence room.

What is the price tag on your integrity? Ralph Waldo Emerson once said, "Money often costs *too* much."

Many times a person over pays for what he gets for nothing.

"Why didn't you take the money?" one of my students asked in my Ethics Class.

"What worries me most," I said to the young officer, "is why you have to ask me why."

THE SUITCASE CONTAINING OVER HALF MILLION DOLLARS, CONFISCATED DURING THE TRAFFIC STOP.

FIGHT IN PROGRESS

Jim and I were in a fight for the heavy weight black belt state judo competition. Jim was the better fighter; he was a world champion in Police Olympic judo competition. I was a pretty good club fighter. Jim was also one of the best officers his federal agency had. He was trusted with the lives of many top officials in our country. He was on his way to the top. Unfortunately, I was on the way to the bottom. Jim flipped me so fast that all I remember was seeing the lights above me as my back hit the mat with a thud. In less than one minute I was in the stands drinking a coke and watching Jim get his medal. He was the best fighter I had ever met and someone I respected as a friend and officer.

Then one day the scandal hit Washington, DC. Several officers were fired from the prestigious organization where Jim worked and they all left in disgrace. "What had they done?" I wondered. "Had they sold sensitive information to the Soviet Union? Taken a million dollars from drug lords? Sold dope from the evidence room?" No, nothing quite so grand. It seems that they had turned in false information on their travel expense forms. "Oh, my," I thought, "to lose one's job and bring disgrace on yourself, family and agency over a travel form."

I guess Webb Hubbell was right when he said, "Fred, corruption starts out small."

A few days after this story broke, I got a call from one of Jim's friends. It seems that my friend, the world class fighter, had lost the battle that meant the most. He was one of the guilty officers.

How are your ethics? Are they 10-4, okay, or are they 10-7, out of service?

SEARCHING FOR THE LESSON

Bad cops and unethical people are everywhere. That means that we must all be concerned about a cure. I close with a poem I rewrote from an old poem called, "The Man in the Glass."

The Cop in the Glass

When the tide finally comes and it's the end of your tour,
The people are gone and the stares are no more,
Take a trip to the mirror and take a look at yourself,
And see what that man has to say.

For it isn't the glitter that you've shared with the badge,
Upon whose judgment you must shine,
For the jury whose verdict counts most in your life,
Is the cop staring back from the glass.

Some people may think you've been a straight, honest cop,
For your ethics they have never seen stray,
But the cop in the glass says he knows that you're scum,
If you can't look him straight in the face.

He's the fellow to please, and the tarnish he'll see,
For he is with you clear up to the end.
And your final reward will be heartache and shame,
If you ever disgrace that cop in the glass.

You may not be a cop, but you can put your own occupation in life in its place. What lessons have you learned from these stories? Would you have to enter a guilty plea to any of the above charges?

LEADERSHIP

ROLL CALL

A famous quotation I love to repeat says that "everything rises and falls on leadership". Your career. Your church. Your home. **Everything** rises and falls on leadership. Our country cries out today for leadership. There are many definitions of leadership. I believe that leadership is about people. Do you have the skills (which can be learned) to lead people toward worthwhile goals, or must you push them toward the mark? The word "leader" would seem to say that you are out in front. You can't push someone forward from the front. My boss recently said that leaders lead people, and managers manage things. In reality, of course, a good manager needs to be a good leader, and a good leader a good manager. What he was saying is that things can be replaced; people can't. Things have no emotions, no desires; people do. To say that leaders are born is the lazy person's way out. There is no need for me to go to classes, read books, or attend seminars. Many will say I just don't have the gift. But leadership does not come free. It is not a gift; it must be earned and learned. You may have become a supervisor or manager because you know someone or you're the boss' son or daughter. You may have even bought your job with a political donation. But leadership can not be given to you or even bought for you. You must earn the title through hard work and by learning people skills and gaining the respect of those you lead. Law enforcement is no different. It cries out for leadership. Take a look at these next three stories and see how you would rank them in leadership skills.

AN ENCOURAGING WORD

Patrol Captain Skinner was at home listening to his police scanner when it all began. I had stopped Mike E. Bonner for reckless driving. Mr. Bonner finally pulled over in the parking lot of a small "get and go" grocery store. I got out of my patrol car and headed for his driver's side door when all of a sudden he put his car in reverse, revved up the engine, squealed his tires and attempted to run over me. I jumped back into my patrol car for protection. As I tried to sit up inside my car, I was pushed back in my seat by the crash. Mr. Bonner was now ramming my car and trying to push my patrol car into the gas pumps that were in the middle of the parking lot. I finally got control of my car before I was pushed into the gas pumps and broke free of Mr. Bonner's car. Mr. Bonner took off at a high rate of speed and the chase was on. I know police chases are looked down on and should only be used in serious cases. I believed this case was serious. This man was trying to kill me. The chase lasted nearly thirty minutes. The final report would say that Mr. Bonner tried to kill me by slowing down and then ramming my car no less than twenty times. At one point I was about to discontinue the chase because I had lost sight of his car; but when I came over the top of a small hill, there was Mr. Bonner waiting for me. I slammed on the brakes and stopped just short of his rear bumper. Then a unique event occurred. He stuck his arm out the window and gave me *the finger,* (his crude sign language was not the unique event), put his car in reverse, and started chasing me backwards. He rammed into my car several more times while we were both going backward and I was trying to get out of his way. He then put his car in drive and started going forward and the forward chase was on again. Enough time had elapsed that a second patrol car had caught up with us and was helping me with the chase. All of a sudden, it began to rain. The road became very slick. Mr. Bonner put on his brakes. I swerved around him to avoid ramming the rear of his car. As I came up beside him, my front bumper got caught on the side of his car. We both started going forward again and were locked onto each other. I'll never forget looking over at Mr. Bonner; he was laughing as hard as he could. I looked down the road and saw a large truck approaching. Mr. Bonner must have seen it, too. He began pushing my car into the path of the truck. As we were driving down the road, my car was still attached to his and it was clear he was trying to kill me by pushing me into the path of the truck. I began to try to push him onto the shoulder of the road. We were pushing each other back and forth when suddenly I heard an explosion and felt my car break free of his. My car finally stopped and I jumped out and discovered what had happened. Mr. Bonner had struck a utility pole along the side of the road which, thank God, had broken me free. My partner's car was unable to stop because of the rain slick highway and had rammed into the back of Mr. Bonner's car. Although, I didn't know until later, one electrical line had broken free and was resting on Mr. Bonner's car and was bouncing off my partner's car. I am told thousands of volts of electricity were going through Mr. Bonner's car as well as my partner's car. Mr. Bonner's car caught on fire and smoke was everywhere. I screamed at Mr. Bonner and my partner to get out of their cars because both vehicles were on fire. Because of the smoke, I could not see the wire on top of Mr. Bonner's car. My partner jumped out of his car and fell to the ground. The two passengers dove out of Mr. Bonner's car. Mr. Bonner then dove out of the front window of his car but his feet got caught on the side of the car. His hands went into a large puddle of water next to the car. I'm told that when that happened, Mr. Bonner became the ground for the electricity which shot throughout his whole body, killing him instantly. Captain Skinner had by now gotten into his patrol car at home and was headed for the scene. When he arrived, he saw quite a mess. My partner was in the ambulance. His heart had stopped beating due to the shock he had received. One man lay dead in the roadway; his two passengers were en route to the hospital. I was sitting beside the road in complete exhaustion. The press were everywhere. Helicopters were overhead. For all I knew, my partner was dying. I had come close to death myself. I heard a police officer who had later arrived at the scene from another jurisdiction ask, "You think it was a justified case for a pursuit?"

I finally looked up and saw what I *hoped* was a friendly face. It was Captain Skinner. Although he didn't have a reputation for being the most pleasant supervisor on the force, I still naively expected he would support me in this tragic situation. I will never forget his words of "encouragement" that day. He approached me while I was still sitting in the grass beside the road. I noticed he had a huge plug of tobacco in his jaw. As he put his hands on his hips, he paused momentarily to make a brief observation of the accident scene. He then bent over, spit tobacco juice, (barely missing me), and said in disgust, "You sure know how to screw up two brand new patrol cars, don't you, kid?"

That's all he said. Then he left the scene. "Thanks, that's just what I needed," I said to myself as I got up and walked to the ambulance to check on my partner.

SEARCHING FOR THE LESSON

The investigation by the sheriff, the prosecuting attorney and internal affairs cleared me and my partner of any wrongdoing. When I began to get praise from these people for a job well done, Captain Skinner changed his attitude. But for me, it was too late for him to come on board. A true leader knows the time to rebuke and the time to encourage. Whether it's a police officer under stress, a child who has flunked out of college, or a spouse who has lost a job, a leader needs first to be concerned about people. The material things will wait. New patrol cars can be bought. Vocational or Technical College may be preferred. One can always find a job, but a broken spirit sometimes can never be mended.

SCENE OF THE INCIDENT SHORTLY AFTER THE FATAL CHASE ENDED. MY PATROL CAR IS THE VEHICLE IN THE RIGHT FRONT. NOTICE THE FALLEN ELECTRICAL WIRE LAYING ACROSS MR. BONNER'S CAR. (LEFT SIDE OF PHOTO)

LEADERSHIP NIGHTMARE

I couldn't believe it was happening again. Another chase. I was dispatched to an armed robbery in progress. When I arrived at the scene, the suspects jumped in their car, took a shot at me, and took off at a high rate of speed. I remember chasing them and thinking - "Not again. Please not another chase like the last one." Then it happened, the rain started (just like the chase in the previous story you read). "Oh, no," I thought, "it's happening again." A passenger in the suspect's car leaned out his window and took another shot at me. This time he didn't miss. The shot shattered my windshield and caused me to crash. I guess I was afraid the car would catch on fire like the car in the last chase I was in. So I jumped out of my car. That, I would soon learn, was a bad decision. As I ran from my patrol car, I heard a pop like a firecracker. Then, I felt it. It felt just exactly as I had heard other officers describe it - as though someone had run a red hot poker through them. "Oh, no," I thought, "I've been shot." I fell to the ground and felt two more bullets go through my body. Then a squeal of tires and they were gone. I lay there in the roadway thinking, "I will not die, if I can get help, I will live." I then reached down to grab my walkie-talkie to call for help. And, as I reached for my radio pouch, it hit me. "They have killed me." I said, "they have killed me." Surprisingly, it wasn't the bad guys I was blaming. It was my department - for as I reached for my radio, I remembered they had taken away all our walkie-talkies for punishment and my radio pouch was empty. I knew then that I would die. And I began to cry.

"Honey, what's wrong?" my wife said. "Honey, are you okay?"

"Huh, what," I said. As I shot straight up from my bed.

"You're crying," she said, "you must have been having a bad dream."

"No, honey," I said, "it was a horrible nightmare."

The nightmare I had was not true. I had not been shot at by an armed robber, but the part about the radio was true. And that's what angers me to this day.

The week before the dream, a rookie police officer had left his walkie-talkie on top of his patrol car. When he pulled out of the parking lot, the radio slid off and he ran over it. Chief Benson was so mad that he told the patrol commanders to pull all walkie-talkies from his division as an example to the rest of us to take better care of our equipment. For many of us, the walkie-talkie was our life line since we didn't have back up in the county that could respond quickly. We protested but in those days, no one protested too loudly. There was no police union or FOP for many of us and we worked at the pleasure of the sheriff. We only got the radios back when our wives sent an anonymous letter to the chief that they were going to the media with the story if radios weren't returned. I'll never forget being so angry at my chief for not thinking any more of our lives than that. I was angry that they had put so much pressure on me, that it made me dream what I did. And the thing I am most angry about is what I did in the dream. To this day, it bothers me that in the dream, I lay there in the middle of the street and cried like a baby. I am haunted still when I think that my supervisor would punish me for something I didn't do and he didn't mind risking my life to save a walkie talkie.

SEARCHING FOR THE LESSON

Leaders would do well to remember they are in a "people" business. While equipment is important, it can easily be replaced.

President George Bush said, "Use power to help people. For we are given power not to advance our own purposes nor to make a great show in the world, nor a name. There is but one just use of power and it is to serve people."

ELECTION NIGHT

All my supervisors were not bad as I have portrayed in the last two stories. I remember Lt. Ray Thomas, who showed up at the scene of the chase that ended in the suspect's death. He told me after he had heard what Captain Skinner had said about the patrol car being wrecked, "Lad, you did a great job. If it had been me, I *wouldn't* have chased him, I'd have just *shot* him!" He was the only shift commander that supported me, that night. And, by the way, I think he was just kidding me about shooting the suspect......*I think he was.*

Chief Tom Oakes is one of the police chiefs I worked for and a good friend. He taught me that, while I wanted to be as professional as the state police or the FBI, I should never forget the heart of his hero, Andy Griffith. Andy had a heart for the citizens of Mayberry.

Sgt. Al Hughes, my jail sergeant, showed me he wasn't afraid to get his hands dirty. "I won't ask you to do anything I won't do," he once told me. He was always willing to help us whether it was booking people in jail or entering a cell to break up a fight. Major John Bowlen inspired me to continue my education, and Captain Ray Wolf hired me and gave me a chance to become a correctional officer which started my career in 1977. I have learned about leadership from all these people.

While I'm not sure I am a good leader, I try. I have been given many awards for leadership. Every governor since I have been in Arkansas has given me a citation for excellence in leadership. In 1994, I was chosen supervisor of the year for the Arkansas Department of Correction. In 1997, I was chosen the Arkansas Boss of the Year from over eight thousand possible state employee supervisor candidates.

What do your employees think about you? They don't have to love you but they should respect you, not out of fear but for your honesty and treatment of them. A deputy told me recently, that if the election was held for his sheriff just from among his employees, he would lose. How would you do in an election? You might be surprised.

SEARCHING FOR THE LESSON

As I said in the beginning of this chapter, leadership is a learned art. A painter must first learn to paint a straight line before he or she can paint a sunset. Some learn more quickly than others, of course. But the art of being a good leader, whether in business or in the home, I believe, is to never put down the brush until you have taken your last breath.

BEING RECOGNIZED BY
GOVERNOR
BILL CLINTON,
GOVERNOR
JIM "GUY" TUCKER,
AND
GOVERNOR
MIKE HUCKABEE
FOR
VARIOUS LEADERSHIP
ACCOMPLISHMENTS.

ARKANSAS
STATE TREASURER,
JIMMIE LOU FISHER
PRESENTING TO ME THE
BOSS OF THE YEAR
AWARD, 1997.

THE KIDS

ROLL CALL

Of all the calls that a police officer must respond to, those calls dealing with children are usually the worst. A police officer in the west once told me that he responded to a call where a child had been left alone in a car. The vehicle became so hot that the child suffocated and died. By the time the child was discovered, her body had exploded. He knew he needed help when this didn't bother him. The evening after this incident, he told me he was at home sitting in his easy chair and began to weep uncontrollably. His wife tried to help him by saying it was okay for him to lose control after what he had been through. "Honey," he said, "I'm not crying for the baby, I'm crying for myself because I can't cry for the baby." When a cop can't cry for the children, he has a serious problem and has become too hard for the job. See how your heart responds to the children from behind the badge.

MAKE YELLOW

Kathy was only three years old. Her mother had warned her that if she wet the bed one more time, she would kill her. She wasn't kidding. On an early spring morning, Kathy went crying to her mother. "Mommy," she said, "I made yellow" - which was her way of saying that she had wet the bed. Her mother grabbed Kathy and her father's belt and began to beat Kathy until, according to the coroner, she tore the flesh off Kathy's back. She then picked up a hot iron and placed it on her baby's back - peeling the flesh off her little body. Then, to make sure she understood the seriousness of her bed wetting, she placed her child in a pot of boiling water until Kathy was dead. Her mother would later claim that she was drunk and remembered nothing about the event.

"But she wasn't so drunk that she couldn't get the belt, plug in the iron, and heat the water," the officer told the jury.

"Objection," the defense attorney screamed. "Yeah, I bet you object," the officer said under his breath.

SEARCHING FOR THE LESSON

Even the most committed anti-capital punishment advocates have told me that in some cases there just may be an exception.

BILLS DUE

Mary came to my office, escorted by one of my detectives. "She wants to tell you something, Chief," the detective said.

"I can't take it anymore," she said. "My old man keeps hurting my little girl. He gets drunk," she said, "and beats us both and makes us do terrible things."

The terrible thing he was forcing them to do was to perform pornographic acts on video; then he would sell the videos to his friends. After a search warrant was issued, we confiscated about fifty tapes from their home, and after viewing them with two detectives, we found the evidence we needed.

Mary's daughter was only eleven years old. The acts I saw on the tapes need not be explained in great detail. I have tried to forget the contents of the videos, but I shall *never* forget the look on the little girl's face, while suffering the unconscionable sexual abuse by her *mother* and father. Hers was a face completely void of all emotion and life. She had the look of the living dead. My heart broke as I watched the physical and mental torture of this innocent child. The mother performed the sexual acts on her own daughter and the father was the director. As the little girl lay there being abused, I noticed her staring directly into the camera. Her eyes were begging someone to rescue her and stop her unspeakable torture, but no one came to her aid.

As the first video ended, I saw both of my detectives crying. The despicable acts revealed on the video were more than any of us could comprehend. I too, wept. We just silently sat there for a few moments until we could regain our composure. Unfortunately, we had only begun the necessary evil of viewing the videos.

"How long has this been going on?" I asked.

"Since she was six," the mother explained.

"Why did you wait so long to report this?" I asked angrily.

"I needed someone to pay the bills," she said.

We arrested both the mother and the father. The little girl was removed from the home and placed in state care.

SEARCHING FOR THE LESSON

As I began to write this story, I did okay. Then I got to the point where I tell about reviewing the videos. I couldn't believe it, but even after some twelve years, I again found myself crying for this little girl. I had to stop writing for a while to get hold of my emotions. I can not read this story out loud, as it still breaks my heart.

I can't begin imagine what emotional damage was done to this innocent child.

I believe Hell will burn the hottest for those who abuse children. Luke 17:2 says, "It would be better for him, that a millstone were hanged about his neck, and he was cast into the sea than he should offend one of these little ones."

LAST CALL

The last call I ever went on as a patrol officer involved a twelve year old boy. When I arrived at his home, his father met me at the door and said that his son was upstairs. When I passed his mother in the dining room, she was screaming and beating her fists on the table. When I entered the young boy's room, I found him lying on the floor in a pool of blood. A pistol was in his right hand and the top of his head was blown apart. I found a suicide note on his bed. In part it read, "Dear Mom, I'm sorry I can't be the kind of boy you want me to be. At last, I'm at peace."

As the detective snapped the pictures and the coroner zipped up the body bag, I remember thinking, "Why, would a twelve year boy kill himself?"

I guess that should be answered by the experts. I'm just glad I won't have to respond to any more calls like this.

SEARCHING FOR THE LESSON

Don't take the problems of the young for granted. Norman Vincent Peale said, "There is no doubt in my mind that mental and spiritual health are the foundation of physical health, harmonious relationships, and a happy and successful life."

John Milton stated, "The mind is it's own place, and in itself can make a heaven of hell, or a hell of heaven."

HUMOR

ROLL CALL

A law enforcement officer's career is not all filled with death and pain. Books and television shows have been written about the funny side of the badge. I recently saw a book at a local book store called the World's Dumbest Crooks.

It's been said that laughter is life's best medicine. For us in law enforcement, a big spoonful of laughter helps us all handle the pains of tragedy that may await on our next call.

WHAT'S IN A NAME?

The following story is both funny and unique. I've heard President Clinton tell it at several state functions.

My good friend and fellow instructor at the Law Enforcement Academy has a very unusual name. His first name is Robin, and his last name is Hood. Robin Hood.

When Robin was a young man about sixteen years old, he had a good friend named Paul. Paul also had an unusual last name. It was Revere. Paul Revere. (Actually spelled Riviere but pronounced Revere.)

One day, as the story goes, Robin and Paul were out for a Saturday night drive. Robin, being a bit heavy footed, was speeding down a country road. In his rear view mirror, he saw a pair of flashing red lights. Robin quickly pulled over and waited for the officer to approach. Shortly, the officer was standing at Robin's car door.

"May I see your driver's license, please," the officer said.

After a nervous search, Robin told the officer, "I must have forgotten it and left it at home."

"What's your name, son?" the officer asked.

"Robin, sir."

"Robin what?"

"Robin Hood, sir."

"Son," the officer said, "don't get smart with me. What's your name?"

"I swear it's Robin Hood."

The officer's jaw began to twitch. The officer quickly looked at Robin's passenger. "What's your name, boy? *And don't you get smart with me."*

“Paul, sir.”

“Paul, what?” the officer asked.

“Paul, uh, Paul, uh, Paul Revere, sir.”

“Oh, a pair of wise guys,” the officer said. “Well, I’m the Sheriff of Nottingham, and you two are going to jail.”

SEARCHING FOR THE LESSON

I searched and searched to find a deep, philosophical and possibly life impacting lesson, in this funny little story. The closest thing to a lesson I found was this: If your name is Robin Hood, don't hang around with people named Paul Revere, or Maid Marion, Little John or Friar Tuck . . . !!

FRIENDS IN HIGH PLACES

A traffic officer hears more excuses and reasons for not giving someone a ticket than most officers. One day an officer pulled over a young woman for speeding. He had been working this section of highway for about a week and was growing tired of all the excuses for traffic violations. The officer asked for the young woman's driver's license. He noticed on the driver's license that she was required to wear corrective lenses (glasses).

"Young lady," the officer said, "I see here on your driver's license that you are supposed to be wearing corrective lenses. I'm going to give you a ticket for not wearing your glasses."

"Oh, no, officer. You don't understand. I have contacts. I don't have to wear my glasses."

The officer, who I'm sure was just joking, said, "Lady, I don't care who you know, you're still getting a ticket."

SEARCHING FOR THE LESSON

Language is a strange world. It is a place where skating on thin ice can get you in hot water!

MIGHTY MAN

It happened one night while I was the guest speaker at a drug free rally for a large church in Pennsylvania. On this night, my past experience as a martial arts student would, unfortunately, shine brightly.

It happened when I was about halfway through my speech. There comes a time when you can just tell that even though your audience is looking straight at you, they're just not hearing a word you're saying. So I decided to use a little trick that I had been taught in an instructor's class. We were advised that if we ever got to a place where our audience was not listening to us or we ran out of things to say, to just yell real loud and hit the podium. What I had forgotten was that this is the same trick my old martial arts teacher had taught me about how to break boards many years ago. Well, I wanted to wake everybody up, so I gave it the "old instructor hit and yell trick", and guess what happened? Yep, you guessed it. I suppose there has never been a better demonstration of podium splitting in the State of Pennsylvania. Master Poe would have been proud. The crowd went into hysterics. Laughter was coming from everywhere. I didn't know what to say or do. The podium was broken completely in half and pieces were laying everywhere. I looked over at the pastor; he was smiling, but not laughing. I'm sure he was not too pleased that I had just broken his favorite pulpit. I then looked back at the congregation and the only thing that I could think to say was, "Now ladies and gentlemen, that is an example of how it must have been when the spirit of the Lord fell upon Samson and he became a mighty man. And remember 'just say no to drugs' or I'll be back!" Oh, well, at least I got their attention.

SEARCHING FOR THE LESSON

You can have great ideas, but if you can't get them across to your audience, your ideas will go nowhere! But I must admit, I may have gotten just a *little* extreme

DISPLAYING TWO OF MY JUDO AWARDS.

ATTENTION........... CALLING ALL CARS:

BE ADVISED WE HAVE AN APB OUT FOR MORE TRUE STORIES AND POEMS FROM ANY..............

Police Officer
Sheriff & Deputy
Correction Officer
Firefighter
Jailer
Bailiff
E.M.T.
Paramedic
Parole Officer
Probation Officer
Dispatcher
Security Personnel
Federal Officer
Military Police
Coroner
Prosecuting Attorney
Search & Rescue Personnel
Fish & Game Officer
Game Warden
Forest & Park Ranger,
and

anyone who works with or volunteers in any of the above professions. The rest of the world may want to read your true stories and poems in one of my future books. Just send your typed and double spaced contributions, along with your name and telephone number to:

FRED CAMPBELL
PO BOX 282
JEFFERSON, AR 72079

If we include your offering in one of our books, you can be sure that you will be credited for your contribution.

***

WORKSHOPS, LECTURES AND SEMINARS

As President of "Motivational Speakers Institute," Mr. Campbell is a highly acclaimed and dynamic public speaker who conducts professional and personal workshops and seminars for business clients, corporations and public audiences across the nation. He is called **"America's Best Storyteller"**. His exciting and electric speaking style is filled with passion and unmatched exuberance. *Some* of his *seminar* topics are: **LEADERSHIP SECRETS, LIFE'S LESSONS FROM BEHIND THE BADGE AND WINNING ATTITUDES.**

For information about booking Mr. Campbell for a speaking engagement or information on how to obtain additional copies of this book contact:

Chief Fred Campbell

PO Box 282

Jefferson, AR 72079

CHIEF FRED CAMPBELL